With love
Dad and Mom
Christmas 1988.

PATH FINDERS
AT WAR

Lancasters of 83 Squadron,
PFF, at dusk, being prepared
for a night operation.

PATH FINDERS
AT WAR
Chaz Bowyer

OL 21

LONDON

IAN ALLAN LTD

First published 1977
Third impression 1987

ISBN 0 7110 0757 8

Published by Ian Allan Ltd, Shepperton, Surrey;
and printed by Ian Allan Printing Ltd at their works
at Coombelands in Runnymede, England

DEDICATION

'*Dusk is our dawn, and midnight is our noon,*
And for the sun we have the silver moon:
We love the darkness, and we hate the light;
For we are wedded to the gloomy night.'

. . . The Night Bombers
P. Bewsher, 1917.

Contents

Introduction

A popular radio programme in America used to open with the invariable phrase, 'There are six million stories in this city. This is just one.' The same might be said about this book. The Path Finder Force – No 8 (PFF) Group, RAF Bomber Command – during its brief existence from August 1942 to December 1945 was a select formation with specific terms of reference, and became the spearhead of Bomber Command's part in the awesome destruction of Germany during the last three years of World War Two. Its air crew members were almost wholly volunteers, and despite the terrifying odds against any individual, or complete crew, ever completing the requisite 60-sorties tour of operations with the PFF, the most feared 'punishment' for PFF members was to be 'sacked' and posted away to another unit. Such was the fierce pride and spirit of dedication to the PFF task.

To tell every man's story is clearly an impossibility. Nor is this book in any sense a history of No 8 (PFF) Group. A full history of the Path Finders has yet to be published, but if this volume can be regarded as a *multum in parvo*, it will then, at least, have achieved the main part of my purpose in compiling it. The contents are simply a sincere attempt to recreate something of the authentic 'atmosphere' of the subject and its place in history. As with previous titles in this series, much of the narrative has come from men with first-hand experience – the men who flew with, or were an integral part of the PFF. They and they alone are best qualified to recount the Path Finder story.

It must also be emphasised that the subject matter herein has been deliberately restricted to No 8 (PFF) Group, RAF Bomber Command. To have attempted to include literally all 'path-finding' units and formations in one, relatively slim volume would have been to do a gross injustice to the broader subject. Thus, and most reluctantly, I have had to omit more than this briefest of mentions of the equally gallant activities of other 'path-finders' in the various air services engaged in 1939-45. These would include an element in the other Bomber Command groups of the RAF; squadrons so employed in the Middle East campaigns; the USAF, the Luftwaffe; et al. Each demands a separate book, or series of volumes, wherein adequate recognition might be given to the men of such formations.

Finally, in this apologia, I should 'declare my interest' in order to avoid possible misconceptions. I was never a member of that gallant company, the PFF; hence I have no parochial bias. This book is simply intended as a sincere tribute to such men – and a small epitaph for the crews who failed to return from the PFF's many operations.

In compiling this volume I have, yet again, been extraordinarily fortunate in the number of individuals who offered help with information and material. However, I could hardly have started it without the invaluable and mighty generosity of two men in particular – Group Captain T G 'Hamish' Mahaddie, DSO, DFC, AFC, C ENG, AFRAES, and Squadron Leader Howard Lees. Hamish, who, to me, epitomises all that the description 'Path Finder' really means, was a constant source of enormous encouragement, material and contacts; and, equally generous with material and whole-hearted support, Howard Lees cheerfully permitted me to pester him on many occasions, and never once failed to meet my importunacy with open-handed hospitality. As the Group Photographic Officer of the PFF his personal contributions to the high efficiency of the force were prodigious. If this book disappoints, let the blame rest entirely on my shoulders – not theirs.

The list of other selfless helpers is long, but the very least I can do is to offer a public word of sincere gratitude for their aid. Foremost, naturally, are the individual contributors whose stories appear within. The old RAF fear of being accused of 'line-shooting' had to be dispelled before I could persuade them to burst into print. To the following individuals I owe a debt of thanks for the various ways in which they assisted me. Mrs Joan Halsey for her permission to quote from the wartime log of her husband, the late Flight Lieutenant A K Halsey; Kathleen Nathan of the Hutchinson publishing group for her ready permission to quote an extract from the superb little book *Pathfinders*, by Wing Commander E W Anderson, OBE, DFC, AFC, published 1947 by Jarrolds (London) Ltd; Philip Q Back, DFC; H F Brundle, DFC; the late Group Captain H E Bufton, DSO, OBE, DFC, AFC; R V Dickeson, DFC; Squadron Leader D H Harrild, DFC; Squadron Leader L G Hind; R B Leigh, DFC; N E Litchfield, DFC; L O Owen; Bruce Robertson; J Shaw; P R Turner; L Woodhead; Wing Commander M A Smith, DFC. And for help with certain photographs, and in other ways, I am indebted to D C Bateman of the Air Historical Branch, MOD; Ted Hine of the Imperial War Museum's Department of Photographs; A W Price; J Richard Smith. A final word of thanks must go to Jimmy Hughes, DFM of the Path Finder Association, and editor of the association's magazine *The Marker*; and Alex Thorne, DSO, DFC, editor of the RAF Association's quarterly magazine *Air Mail* – both of whom generously 'spread the word' on my behalf.

Norwich, 1976   *Chaz Bowyer*

Prologue

Left: Scampton scene on August 15th, 1942, as 83 Squadron personnel prepare to move to Wyton. At right is the main guardroom; whilst the camouflaged building top left is Station Headquarters. 83 was one of the four founder-units of the PFF on this date.

Below: Another founder-member of the PFF was 35 Squadron, previously based at Linton-on-Ouse, York. This particular Halifax, W7676, TL-P, was also one of the PFF's earliest casualties, being lost during a raid on Nuremburg on the night of August 28/29th, 1942./*Charles E Brown*

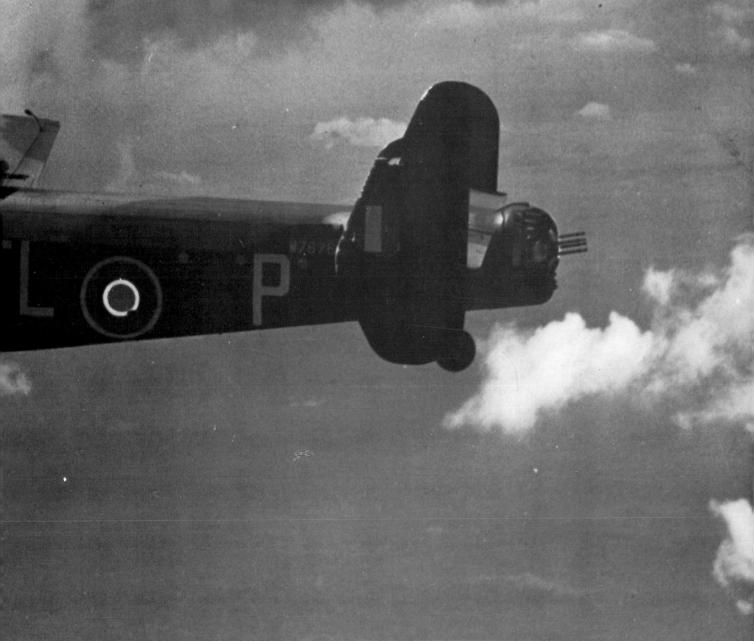

The basic concept of locating and marking a target in advance of any bombing force had its small beginnings in the 1914-18 war in the air. In 1916, for example, Lieutenant R B Bourdillon, a pilot of No 27 Squadron, Royal Flying Corps in France, evolved a simple scheme of target location by measuring – as accurately as contemporary crude instrumentation permitted – a time and distance to any target; even in cloud conditions where ground visibility was nil. In the early years of World War Two the Luftwaffe used a system of radio beams to indicate distance to a precise bomb release point over a target; whilst by 1941, GEE-equipped bombers of No 3 Group, RAF Bomber Command were undertaking similar operations over Europe. Within the RAF, however, there was no co-ordinated scheme whereby a main bomber stream could be guided accurately to any target, and that target precisely 'marked' for the main force to bomb. Allied to the contemporary RAF policy of 'area bombing' – a deliberate policy of intimidation of the German civil population by destruction of large areas of urban communities – precision bombing of specific targets was seldom achieved with any great success.

The initial 'champion' of a separate target-finding force within Bomber Command was Group Captain S O Bufton, DSO, DFC, who in early 1942 was Deputy Director of Bomber Operations at the Air Ministry. An experienced operational bomber captain, Syd Bufton had recognised the paramount importance of accurate navigation as a pre-requisite to any significant bombing offensive, and was adamant in his belief that Bomber Command needed to concentrate on achieving precision, rather than continue its area bombing offensive. As evidence for his views he pointed out to higher authority that in eight raids against Essen, from March 8th to April 12th, 1942, almost 90 per cent of the aircraft despatched had released their bomb loads from five to 100 miles away from the actual designated target. His suggested solution was to create a formation of six squadrons, based 'in close proximity to each other', and manned by normal crews, but leavened by the influx of 40 of the best and most experienced operational crews then available within the command.

Gathering support for his ideas amongst other ex-operational senior officers at Air Ministry, Bufton presented his suggestions to the Air Officer Commanding-in-Chief (AOC-in-C), Bomber Command, Air Chief Marshal Arthur Harris. He promptly met with total opposition to the implementation of any form of separate force within the command. 'Butch' Harris – his affectionate nickname amongst his crews – though not in disagreement with the principle of having selected crews to spearhead raids, was nevertheless strongly opposed to any form of 'elite corps' in his command. Instead he preferred to have specific squadrons within each group, nominated by group commanders, to act as 'Raid Leaders' (Harris's descriptive title). Paradoxically, Harris's rooted objection to 'elite' formations later changed when he had 617 Squadron created; and hardly accords with his personal attitude to No 5 Group to which he gave virtual autonomy throughout the remainder of the war.

Pursuant to his own ideas for specially selected crews for target-finding duties within each squadron, Harris, in a letter to the Chief of Air Staff, dated June 12th, 1942, pressed for a unique emblem for these men – '. . . an RAF eagle, to be worn below medal ribbons.' This gilt badge was later to be the proudly-worn award of every man who qualified as a Path Finder. Only two days later Harris received from the CAS a letter which amounted to a direction to form a separate formation for target location duties. The letter ended by saying that it was, '. . . the opinion of the Air Staff that the formation of a special force with a role analagous to that of the reconnaissance battalion of an Army division would immediately open up a new field for improvement, raising the standard and thus the morale which could not fail to be reflected throughout the whole force.' Accepting the inevitable, Harris immediately pressed for the right to special promotion for members of the proposed force, in view of their stipulated extended tour of operations from the normal Bomber Command's standard of 30 sorties to 60 sorties in the new formation. Opposition to this came immediately from the Treasury, but was overcome, and on August 11th, 1942, Harris was officially directed to proceed with the establishment of the new force.

To lead the new formation Harris selected an Australian-born wing commander, Donald Bennett. In doing so Harris could hardly have picked a man more suited to the task. A navigation expert without peers; widely experienced in flying all types of aircraft from fighters to flying boats and heavy bombers; an operational bomber captain who had already commanded Nos 77 and 10 Squadrons; Bennett was blessed with an intelligence far above the ruck, and a memory for detail which might be termed phenomenal. Equally, his single-minded dedication to any given task brought him few friends in the RAF hierarchy and certain government circles. He was then just 32 years old, thereby combining relative youth with vast and, most important, recent experience – a combination unique amongst his contemporary group commanders in Bomber Command. From the date of his

PATH FINDER BOSS – Air Vice-Marshal Donald Bennett, CB, CBE, DSO, who, at 32 years of age, took command of the newly-formed PFF, and continued to lead the force until the end of the war in Europe.

PFF HQ STAFF – the nucleus of Bennett's headquarters staff at Wyton, 1942-43. Bennett is seated centre; fifth from left is Group Captain (later Air Commodore, CBE) C D C Boyce, the Group administration officer; fourth from left is Wing Commander Ray Hilton, DSO, DFC.

official appointment Bennett never ceased to demand the utmost from those under his command in the prosecution of the war against Germany – and gave no less of himself. An anecdote * probably illustrates, in the simplest terms, his entire attitude to the war and its successful conclusion. Witnessing one of his station commanders conduct a minor disciplinary charge against an airman, who had been accused of crossing the grass instead of using a concrete pathway en route to his place of work; Bennett asked which was the *quickest* and most direct route for the airman to take. He was told, 'Across the grass'. Bennett then made it crystal clear to those present that he would personally punish any man *not* taking the quickest and most direct route to his workplace.

The embryo Path Finder Force came into being officially on August 15th, 1942, when its headquarters was established at RAF Wyton, Huntingdonshire. It comprised just four units: 7 Squadron (Short Stirlings) based at Oakington; 35 Squadron (Handley Page Halifaxes) at Graveley; 83 Squadron (Avro Lancasters) which was transferred to Wyton from Scampton on that date; and 156 Squadron (Vickers Wellingtons) at the satellite airfield at Warboys. A fifth unit, 109 Squadron (DH Mosquitos) was, for the moment, only 'attached' to the PFF, based at Wyton, and concerned mainly with development and operational testing of the new OBOE radar equipment. The PFF at this stage came under the aegis of No 3 Group, Bomber Command for all administrative purposes, but was directly answerable to the AOC-in-C, Harris. Bennett was promoted to Group Captain to

command the PFF initially, and when, on January 8th, 1943, the force was elevated in status to become a separate group, No 8 (PFF), he was accordingly further promoted to Air Commodore, and eventually to Air Vice-Marshal.

In terms of equipment the new force was a polygot mixture of aircraft types, using outdated 1940-41 aids to bombing and navigation; thus it was unable to impose any great improvement in navigational accuracy for the first few months of its career. Nevertheless, ·by the use of fresh ideas on target marking

and bombing, it began slowly to achieve more concentrated bombing by main force bomber streams. Led by Hal Bufton (brother of Syd), 109 Squadron's Mosquitos flew the first operational trials of OBOE on December 20th, 1942, which though not entirely successful were to be the harbinger of future great improvement. In January 1943 two other new inventions had their first testing operationally. On January 16/17th Berlin was the objective when target-indicating ground-marker bombs (TI's) were first used; and on the night of January 30th, Hamburg was

venue for the initial use of H2S-equipped bombers By the late summer of that year the Path Finders were able to claim tremendous precision in marking of targets, and Bomber Command's main force squadrons at last began to show that their gallant efforts were not in vain.

In June 1943 Bennett moved his head-quarters from Wyton to the nearby Castle Hill House, Huntingdon; whilst in April two

Pathfinder by AVM D C T Bennett, published Muller, 1953.

Lancaster R5620, OL-H (nearest) of 83 Squadron heads a taxying line of aircraft, preparing for take-off.

more units had been added to his force, when 405 Squadron RCAF moved into a new airfield at Gransden Lodge; and 97 Squadron (Lancasters) was based at Bourn. In early June two Mosquito units joined 109 in the OBOE aspect of PFF operations, these being 105 and 139 Squadrons, both based at Marham. A fourth Mosquito unit, 627 Squadron, was added in November 1943; to be joined on January 1st 1944 by a fifth, 692 Squadron. Continuing its gradual expansion to meet its ever-increasing responsibilities, the PFF received two heavy bomber units in the new year; 635 Squadron (Lancasters) in March; and 582 Squadron in April. In the latter month Bennett was suddenly faced with a fait accompli by No 5 Group, whose commander, ever-restless for new ideas, and having an ever-sympathetic backing from his AOC-in-C, was 'given' three of the PFF's squadrons, Nos 83, 97 and 627, in order to pursue 5 Groups esoteric notions of pathfinding and target marking. Bennett's only 'replacement' was a fresh Mosquito unit, 571 Squadron in April; and in August 1944 yet another unit, 608 Squadron joined the force. The 'loss' of three trained, pioneer PFF squadrons was a severe blow to Bennett. Although all three were officially only attached to 5 Group, in the event they remained with that group for the rest of the war, albeit with crews that remained fiercely loyal to the PFF. By January 1945 four more Mosquito squadrons – 128, 142, 162 and 163 – joined the PFF. All Mosquito units by then had formed into what Don Bennett titled the Light Night Striking Force (LNSF), and their contribution to both the PFF and Bomber Command was prodigious. Capable of carrying a 4,000 lb HE HC blast bomb – the so-called 'Cookie' – to targets as far-ranging as Berlin, the Mosquitos came to be regarded by the German population as seriously as any other bomber.

In May 1945 a totally ruined Germany finally surrendered, and the PFF was able to take stock of its three years of struggle. It had flown an overall total of 50,490 individual sorties (including the LNSF effort) against some 3,440 targets). The cost in human lives had been grievous. At least 3,727 members – roughly the equivalent aircrew strength of 20 Lancaster squadrons – had been killed on operations; whilst many hundreds more had been wounded and/or crippled. This tragic figure represented about one-sixth of Bomber Command's fatal casualties throughout the entire war. On May 12th, 1945, Don Bennett – his task completed – was succeeded in command of the force by Air Vice-Marshal John R Whitley; and on December 15th, 1945, No 8 (PFF) Group, RAF Bomber Command, was officially disbanded.

Airborne view of another 83 Squadron Lancaster, R5852, OL-Y. An ex-207 Squadron aircraft, 'Y' was eventually written off when it overshot the runway at Condover on September 10th, 1942. By 1944 the PFF had only Lancasters as its heavy bomber equipment./*Imperial War Museum*

LANCASTER MK I
MERLIN.
JAN 1944

Above left: Refined Lanc – JB675, originally a Mk III but converted to a Mk VI, fitted with Rolls Royce Merlin 85 engines (each of 1635 hp), and then used extensively for further engine experiments. It saw service with 635 Squadron; while other Mk VI's were used by 7 Squadron./*Crown Copyright*

Far left: CONFIDENCE TRICK – Mosquito 3.XVI, ML963, 8K-K of 571 Squadron, of the Light Night Striking Force, PFF, modified ('fat belly') to enclose a 4,000lb HC 'Cookie' bomb; demonstrates its crew's confidence in having one engine feathered 'out', despite the war load./*Charles E Brown*

Above: RUHR EXPRESS – Lancaster B.X, KB700, the first Canadian-built Lanc, which joined 405 Squadron RCAF at Gransden Lodge, and flew two ops before being transferred to 419 Squadron. With the latter unit it completed 47 more ops but was destroyed in a crash at Middleton St George on its return from Nuremburg, January 2nd/3rd, 1945. With 405 Squadron it was coded LQ-Q./*Imperial War Museum*

Left: Don Bennett (left) and Group Captain 'Johnny' Fauquier, OC 405 Squadron RCAF, standing in front of Lancaster KB700, 'Ruhr Express'.

Above left: Halifaxes of 35 Squadron and their crews being inspected by an Indian VIP at Wyton on October 22nd, 1942. Front rank is the air crew, while behind them the aircraft's ground crew.

Left: Lancasters of 83 Squadron also receive the keen attention of the Indian VIP, October 22nd, 1942, at Wyton. Third from left is Wing Commander R W P Collings, DFC.

This page: ROYAL VISITORS – May 26th, 1943, when HM King George VI and HM Queen Elizabeth inspected RAF Wyton.

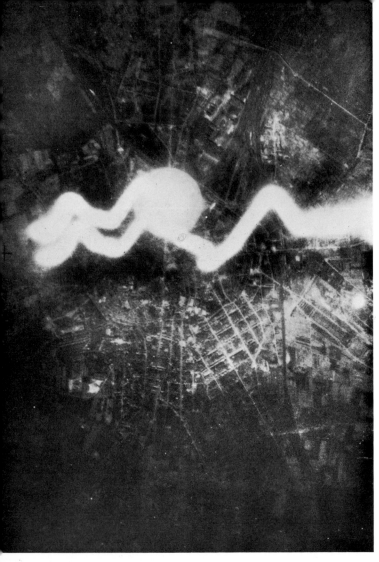

Left: The highest night photo of the war – a view of Osnabruck taken from 36,000 ft by Mosquito 'Z' of 105 Sqn, PFF on the night of April 18/19th, 1944./*Crown copyright*

Above: An attack on Domburg on September 23rd, 1944, viewed from 22,000 ft by Fg Off Thomas in Mosquito 'V' of 109 Squadron. In centre, four markers can be seen descending./*Crown copyright*

Below: AFTERMATH – just one small section of the bombing destruction at Essen, as seen on May 18th, 1945.

Right: AFTERMATH – all that was left of Heligoland in May 1945; testimony to the precision and awesome weight of the Allied bombing.

Below: Headquarters PFF in December 1944.
Front row, L-R: Sqn Ldrs Barnes; Howard; Harrison; Ashley; Whitbread; Jeffreys; H Lees; Mr Jukes; Sqn Ldr Hastings; Wg Cdr Carver; Sqn Ldrs Sellars; Johnson; Smith; Walker; Wood; Major Mullock.
2nd row: Wg Cdrs Thomas; Finn; Barton; Bagnald; McMillan; Shepherd; Burns; Air Cdre Boyce; AVM Don Bennett; Gp Capts White; Sarsby; Wg Cdrs Rose; Rathbone; Ralston; McGown; Deacon; Lt-Colonel Wood.
3rd row: Sqn Ldrs Thorpe; Elliott; Hacking; Baldwin; Flt Lt Barnicott; Flt Off McEvoy; Sqn Off Shaw; Sect Off Whitworth; Sqn Ldrs Vernon; Snow; Flt Lts Rogers; Watkins; Grainger; Sqn Ldr Draycup; Wing.
4th row: Flt Lts Parrott; Giles; Sect Offs Proctor; Sanders; Pollock; Flt Off Gibbs; Bannatyne; Sect Offs Barker; Ashdown; Pierson; Randall; Flt Lt Taylor.
Back row: Flt Lt Mann; Fg Offs McLellan; Targett; Plt Off Lee; Flt Lts Wilson; Barnes; Semple; Caldwell; Jones; Turner; James; Plt Offs Goodwin; Herdson; Flt Lt Harrold; Fg Off Robertson.

In the Beginning

CASUALTY – Lancaster
B.III, LM418, PG-S, of 619
Squadron which was
destroyed in a crash-landing
at Woodbridge, on
returning from the ill-fated
Nuremburg raid of March
30th/31st, 1944. Its crew,
Sgt J Parker as skipper,
survived the crash, but were
all killed in action later./
Imperial War Museum

With the exception of Don Bennett, probably no man is more widely known in the context of the Path Finders than Group Captain Thomas Gilbert Mahaddie, DSO, DFC, AFC, C ENG, AFRAES – 'Hamish'. An ex-Halton aircraft apprentice, Hamish rose to the dizzy heights the hard way, via leading aircraftman, sergeant pilot, pre-1939, to commissioned rank and a career in heavy bombers which extended throughout the war. His most remembered role in the PFF was as the man who, more than any other individual, was directly reponsible for initial selection and transfer of the 'right' men for the force. In all he 'recruited' – by fair means or, on occasion, 'foul' – nearly 19,000 individual PFF crew members. Equally, he was largely responsible for imbuing so many newcomers to the PFF with the 'Path Finder Spirit' – an intangible quality of dedication to the task which, in Hamish in particular, continues to burn with a fervour almost tantamount to a religion. An operational bomber pilot from the earliest RAF sorties over Germany in 1939-40, his account of his personal experiences sets the scene for the initial formation of the PFF and the later massive effort undertaken by RAF Bomber Command. Possibly his best known 'trade marks' were his invariable answer to all queries and problems, 'It's nae bother, laddie'; and his nickname 'Hamish'. The latter was acquired in 1933, in Baghdad, when he

purchased an Arab blue roan 'with legs like a Tiller girl', and named it Hamish. Immediately accused by fellow pilots of bearing a distinct resemblance to his steed, Mahaddie has always maintained that this was a gross insult – to the pony. 'It was a damned good-looking pony', he insists . . .

The first I ever heard of 'path finding' was after briefing in June 1940 when most Whitley crews in 4 Group, Bomber Command, averaged 20-30 sorties a month after the German breakthrough in the Low Countries. Fg Off 'Jimmy' Marks of 77 Squadron (later, Wg Cdr J H Marks, DSO, DFC, killed whilst OC 35 Squadron PFF) got a few of us together and suggested that we made a time-and-distance run from the seemingly everlasting fires of Rotterdam to the target – a large troop concentration, some 35 miles away. It was a relatively easy business to navigate from Spurn Head to the Dutch coast since the glow of Rotterdam could be seen 100 miles away. Marks suggested that after a careful time-distance run from the centre, we could all drop a flare and at the same time fire a red Very Light. The interesting thing about this – in my experience the very first co-ordinated attempt to find a target – was that despite the assurance of all the enthusiasts to the scheme, one Plt Off Leonard Cheshire included, that the run was made with great care, not one of the dozen or more taking part in the quite unofficial effort claimed to have ever seen *one* of the others' flares or Very lights. This occasion was really under ideal conditions, from an easily-defined startpoint and with no opposition. An afterthought but one which may be taken as a portent of the future was that Marks was not deterred by this initial failure. He then *selected* crews for his next experiment, and reduced the numbers to the four best *navigators* in the squadron. It should be remembered that the navigator at that period was also the second pilot. I considered mine was as good as any on the station – he was included. On this occasion the timed run was made with a stopwatch, all compasses had been re-swung and the ASI recalibrated. At the end of the run from Rotterdam, and within a five seconds period, four flares and four Very lights were visible in a radius of approximately three miles, and one flare had pinpointed the target – a large, distinctly-shaped wood concealing troops and armour. At once more flares were identifying the target area and a fair concentration of bombs directed on the aiming point. Ths was confirmed by the immediate reaction from the ground. The time, it should be recalled, was June 1940.

It was not until the advent of GEE (first tried operationally in August 1941, but not

TOP BRASS – AVM Bennett; MRAF Lord Trenchard; Lord Cherwell, in the Wyton officers' Mess.

brought into more general use until March 1942) that *selected* crews were to be given an opportunity to lead non-GEE aircraft to the target by dropping flares on GEE for identification, and sticks of incendiaries for indication, for the lesser-experienced crews to aim their bombs. Little had been learned and at best Bomber Command was only able to leave an estimated three per cent of its lifted weight within five miles of any target. Despite the gallantry and 'press-on' spirit, the bomber offensive was a dismal failure. Thus ended 1941.

Seen purely through the eyes of a bomber captain, the year 1942 saw the awakening of the 'sleeping giant', but although no dramatic results ensued in the first half of the year, save the 'Thousand Plan' (surely the most well conceived confidence trick of the entire war . . .), hope for the future was clearly manifest. The most pertinent thing was the advent of Arthur Harris as the new C-in-C. His arrival at the 'Petrified Forest' (Bomber Command HQ) coincided with the publication of the Lindemann Report – one of the most deadly denunciations of the only serious offensive we were able to mount against the enemy. Whilst the Lindemann 'scourge' had had a devastating effect on the staff at Bomber Command, the Directorate of Bomber Operations at Air Ministry were under no false illusions as to how able the command was in

striking their targets. Moreover, since the admirable 'con trick' of the 'Thousand Plan' they had been extremely active in a certain field; talked about by a few experienced bomber squadron commanders, notably Wg Cdrs 'Willie' Tait, Charles Whitworth, Syd Bufton, and of course 'Jimmy' Marks, who as bomber pilots, flight and squadron commanders, knew where the great weight ended up and, more important, knew why. This select cell and others knew the most experienced 'bomber barons' who had endured nearly three years of bombing, but were now with a 'three-ringed' voice. The most active of these well-disciplined rebels occupied the same office in Air Ministry and were all agreed that the basic cause of our dismal failure to date was *navigation*. Discounting the gallantry and the will to 'press on', if in the face of all the efforts of the enemy – his ack-ack defences, searchlights, decoy targets and, most lethal, ever-increasing fighter 'boxes' – we simply could not find and destroy, the task was virtually impossible in the face of such odds. Thus, this 'think tank' at Air Ministry started talking about a Target-Finding Element, which evolved into a Target Marking Force and, ultimately, a Path Finder Force.

Long before the actual birth of PFF in August 1942, the concept of the Target Finding/Marking Force was well received by the hard-pressed crews but, oddly enough,

GONGS – Group Captain 'Hamish' Mahaddie collects four awards at Buckingham Palace, early 1943.

ROYAL AIR FORCE

PATH FINDER FORCE

Award of
Path Finder Force Badge

This is to certify that

ACTING WING COMMANDER T.G. MAHADDIE DSO.DFC.AFC.
44456.

having qualified for the award of the Path Finder Force Badge, and

having now completed satisfactorily the requisite conditions of

operational duty in the Path Finder Force, is hereby

Permanently awarded the Path Finder Force Badge

Issued this 11th day of **APRIL** in the year 1943 A.D.

Air Officer Commanding, Path Finder Force.

not by the staff at Bomber Command. It took many months to get the staff to evaluate the possibilities of such a scheme. We are told the new C-in-C vetoed the suggestion from the outset and, in the absence of evidence from the archives, this is surely inconsistent with his demand for the agreed build-up of the command, his determination to shed the twin-engined bomber in favour of four-engined Stirlings, Halifaxes and Lancasters; and his bitter and never-ending fight with the Navy (and to a lesser extent with the Army) about the 'milking' of his command. It should be remembered that 'Butch' Harris inherited a virtually bankrupt concern, achieving very little and suffering appalling casualties. The incredible thing at this 'halfway' stage was that crew morale was as high as it was. This was due to many reasons but, in my view, mainly to the excellent field rank officer – the flight and squadron commander – and in no small degree to the basic training of air crews, starting with the Empire air schools in Canada and Rhodesia.

The sadly-lacking mainspring of the entire offensive was the slow build-up of planned routing and the lack of any scientific devices to assist navigators and bomb-aimers. It is extremely odd to reflect today that whilst the boffins managed to save the country in 1940 with radar in the Battle of Britain, no parallel device was being developed to help Bomber Command. There was a scientific hiatus and it took the Lindemann Report and the prodding of the C-in-C to trigger off an effort in this direction. GEE was an excellent start, but soon negated by jamming. It did, however, greatly assist in the concentration of bombers en route to the target and was invaluable in getting aircraft back in conditions of bad weather. GEE's most important occasion was perhaps the Thousand Plan, when nearly 1,000 aircraft passed through the target area in a little over 40 minutes. Taking the Köln raid as one of the most significant landmarks in the bombing offensive, the enormous success of the Thousand Plan ('con trick' or master-minding), it proved beyond doubt that strategic bombing was a war-winning possibility. The 600 acres devastated in Köln – unfortunately not repeated in the other two Thousand Plan targets due to bad weather – only served to prove that new thinking in Bomber Command tactics was still largely influenced by the weather over the target. If nothing else, Köln started, or rather, revised a completely new concept, a new approach, a desperate look at the bombing offensive. By laborious steps, Köln was followed by a renewal of efforts by those at Air Ministry to get the command interested in some form of co-ordinated system of concentration of our bomber streams in time

through the target and, more important, concentration of damage on the aiming point.

The Air Ministry believed that fundamentally it was a question of pure navigation. Quite unofficially, it had also discovered the man for the job, Don Bennett. He was recognised internationally as a superb pilot, with a host of 'firsts' in world aviation; but most important was the undisputed fact that he was an outstanding navigator. He was operational manager of the Atlantic Ferry – in itself an 'impossible task' according to many Service pundits – which had reached an unbelievable degree of success, and in the depths of a deadly winter. Still unofficially, he was approached and, almost clandestinely, invited to Air Ministry where his views on navigation and projected bomber tactics were eagerly given full scope by those who believed that unless we could sustain regular 'Kölns' the strategic offensive could well lose its shot in the arm engendered by the Thousand Plan, and be lost to the Navy and Army, where it would be misdirected and dissipated.

The scene was therefore set for Air Ministry to sell the concept, with a ready-made commander, to Bomber Command. At first the ploy as presented was rejected out of hand. Later the Air Council insisted on the plan being given a try. The C-in-C, Harris, is

Left: BADGES – the standard form awarding its owner a 'permanent' PFF gilt badge, signed personally by AVM Bennett. To achieve this award all PFF members were required to pass a number of searching 'trade tests', in addition to satisfying various stringent operational qualifications at several levels.

Below: Wing Commander J H 'Jimmy' Marks, DSO, DFC./*Imperial War Museum*

believed to have said on receiving the directive, '. . . this is one more occasion where a commander in the field is dictated to by junior officers at the Ministry . . .' It is difficult to understand why the bomber staff was so reluctant to accept the ministerial direction. We are told that the main reason given was the 'weakening' of squadrons by withdrawing the best crews. Nevertheless, after much procrastination, all of which still remains clouded under a veil of 'security', a Path Finder Force was officially formed on August 15th, 1942, and its first commander was Grp Capt D C T Bennett DSO (later, Air Vice-Marshal, CB, CBE DSO) who was officially appointed on July 5th.

Once the formation of PFF was a fait accompli, and apparently against the personal wishes of the Bomber C-in-C and most of his group commanders, the bomber groups were instructed to send selected *volunteer* crews to a squadron 'recruited' by each group and, thereafter, each squadron would be supported by its parent group. Thus, at the outset, 1 Group raised 156 Sqn (Wellingtons); 3 Group, 7 Sqn (Stirlings); 4 Group, 35 Sqn (Halifaxes); and 5 Group, 83 Sqn (Lancasters). By the end of the war PFF comprised eight Lancaster squadrons and 12 Mosquito

units, plus the Met Flight Mosquitos and the PFF Navigation Training Unit. The early problems of the PFF gave its critics much to enjoy since the force was Path Finder in name only. The four initial squadrons, each with a different type of aircraft, had essentially different operational capacities. The one redeeming feature was that groups initially did select good crews, many of them being second-tour types. All the original crews were expected to volunteer for 45 sorties. By and large this meant in effect that each PFF crew would start about a full Bomber Command tour of 30 sorties. Very few, in fact, claimed the 'let-out' and 60 sorties was nearer the average. This incredible sense of duty should be considered against the average sortie life of air crews in the command, which was never higher than 12 and, at one period, as low as eight sorties per crew. Whilst 100 sorties was quite normal in PFF Mosquitos particularly in the OBOE squadrons, several 'heavy bomber barons' did achieve over 100 sorties, and all in Western Europe.

Some very bad-luck cases come to mind, of apparently indestructible characters who were 'chopped' on their last few sorties – 97th or 98th. Two that seemed particularly sad cases were Sqn Ldr D B 'Danny' Everett, DFC of

Above left: Up front – a Short Stirling pilot in his seat, ready to go. 7 Squadron, Oakington./*Flight International*

Left: Preparation of a 7 Squadron Stirling at Oakington./*Flight International*

Above: 'C-for-Colander' – Short Stirling R9257, MG-C, of 7 Sqn, Oakington, with its crew, skippered by Wg Cdr 'Hamish' Mahaddie, DSO, DFC, AFC, Czech MC. Shortly after this photo was taken, the Stirling and its crew raided Cologne on February 1st, 1943, and returned with 174 cannon shell holes as the result of a determined attack by a Junkers 88 night fighter. This whole crew was due to attend an investiture at Buckingham Palace to collect a total of eleven decorations, but on their first trip without Mahaddie as skipper were all lost in action.

Alec Panton Cranswick, DSO, DFC, who was killed over Villeneuve St Georges on the night of July 4/5th, 1944, when skippering Lancaster ND846, TL-J of 35 Squadron, PFF – his 104th operational sortie. It was to Alec Cranswick that AVM Don Bennett dedicated his own biography, 'Pathfinder'.

again to do an extended tour as Path Finders. Although originally we demanded experienced crews, many actually started their operations with PFF. These I personally selected at training schools, generally those with 'Distinguished' passes. After the initial flush of good intentions by the groups, within three months there began a steady deterioration in the standard or crew replacements. In many cases they were not even volunteers. After a further period of three months or so Don Bennett appointed me Group Training Inspector – I became virtually a 'horse thief'. My function was to tour the squadrons daily, using the previous evening's raid as my theme, to explain the difficulties and, in general, to make contact with the Main Force. And I suppose, to make a plea on the spot for greater support in the shape of the best crews, because the best was only just good enough. Another source of crews was the instructional staff at flying and navigation training schools. In my endless lectures to the training groups I charged a 'fee' – two tour-expired instructors! A great number of the OBOE pilots were in fact Blind Approach Training (BAT) instructors, and the hurdle was 1,000 hours on a BAT Flight – the relationship to PFF work here being too obvious to detail.

Possibly the main strength of the PFF lay in the hotch-potch of nationalities. Approximately half the force were from the Commonwealth – Aussies, Canadians, New Zealanders, South African, Rhodesian, and even from as far afield as Hong Kong, Fiji and the West Indies. This all made for healthy competition. I have, in recent years, got into a deal of trouble in certain Commonwealth countries by claiming that an *all*-Canadian or Australian squadron was not as good as a 'mixed' squadron. In fact I have gone further and said a 'mixed' crew was, in my view, infinitely better than *any* 'national' crew. One of the reasons, possibly, for the high proportion of Commonwealth crews was my established policy of spreading my selection 'net' as widely as I could in view of the poor co-operation of the groups at this end. I literally plagued the various HQ's in London, the Aussies at Kodak House et al. I was able to have the pick of excellent crews practically on the dockside as they arrived in the UK. For one example, an excellent 'seam' of Dutchmen was 'worked'. These were all Dutch naval pilots, not particularly experienced but the lack of hours was more than compensated by their almost embarrassing zest for flying. Amongst the first of these was Erik Hazelhoff, at one time Naval Aide to Queen Wilhelmina, and who held the Dutch VC on arrival in PFF. He was the 'bait' that brought many Dutch pilots and navigators to our Mosquito squadrons.

35 Sqn, who was killed on March 7th, 1945, on his 99th sortie. Everett, who had been *ordered* to take a rest after 98 trips, was testing aircraft at the group maintenance units when he heard there was a spare aircraft going begging at his old squadron. Without mentioning it to anyone, he took a scratch crew – and was posted 'Missing, believed killed'. But if Everett's 'chop' was a severe blow, Alec Cranswick's death on July 5th, 1944 ended a living legend. Cranswick was the perfect Englishman – quiet and retiring, but as a bomber captain in an exclusive class of his own. He had done nearly 60 sorties in the Middle East before he came to PFF, and his total trips are somewhat obscure, but it was certainly not less than 137 – Don Bennett, in his book *Pathfinder*, credits him with 143; while Cranswick's biographer merely credits him with 107. Few bomber crews – if in fact any – exceeded this total and certainly not in heavy bombers.

One of the most fascinating aspects of the Path Finders was its attraction for 'characters'. The very nature of the force seemed to beckon the most unusual types. The very mandate of PFF was that crews *had* to volunteer. Which meant in effect that they were volunteering twice – first as air crew and then, if selected,

Halifax HR926, TL-L of 35 Squadron PFF – the 'personal' aircraft of Alec Cranswick, and bearing his family coat of arms as an insigne just below his cockpit./*Ministry of Defence (Air)*

Amongst other nationals was an outstanding Norwegian, Major Christie – now a general in Norway's air force. A host of Americans served, thinly disguised in RCAF uniforms. These were first-rate 'press-on' types. One, a Texan, would never wear the issue flying boots but preferred the cowboy type complete with high heels! It took the whole of his crew to hold him on a table whilst I got a hacksaw and cut at least two inches off his fancy boots – though, somehow, he managed to get them restored. My objection to his high heels was that he would do himself a mischief if he had to bale out . . . An interesting aspect concerning my widely-flung net for Path Finders was that groups after a short while sent crews who had not volunteered to join PFF and, in many cases, had made a nuisance of themselves. By mid-1943 it was made very clear to the Main Force groups that their 'selection' was not acceptable as we were sending more crews back than we were keeping. About this time I noticed that those crews who consistently got aiming point pictures on the bomb plots issued by Bomber Command HQ after each raid were never selected for PFF. In my lecture tours round the squadrons I sought these crews out and, almost without exception, found they had in fact volunteered

for PFF but had their applications rejected. It was a very simple matter to reverse this procedure – generally after some unpleasantness with the appropriate squadron commander.

When PFF had a regular flow of sound, keen material, and the PFF Navigation Unit was in full swing, we saw the steady development of tactics geared to the constant production of new and better 'stores' – target indicators (TI's), hooded flares, and many other innovations; all of which was more than matched by the improvement in navigational techniques. Whilst all this was going on, the enemy night defences were, of course, more than keeping pace with our ever changing methods. It is true to say that the German night fighter dictated the tactics we were forced to adopt. It was a critical struggle – a battle of wits between ourselves and the Luftwaffe night fighters, with the edge always in favour of the Germans. Occasionally we had a trouble-free raid – Dresden, for example. We were never given any long period free from a fight from the coast to a target and back to the coast.

Happily, there were few disasters like the Nuremberg raid of March 30/31, 1944. Of 782 aircraft which set out, we lost 96 which failed to return, some 74 badly damaged which reached England – 22 of these being write-offs after crash-landing and burning out. The total loss of these aircraft and crews was the bitterest blow Bomber Command had to suffer in the entire war, and it is difficult to understand why it happened. Normally the PFF planned the route, which took account of any factors such as the avoidance of heavily defended areas, the upper winds etc. The usual 'dog-legs' associated with a bomber raid were inserted into the route to give a false impression of the true destination. The Mosquito Light Night Striking Force carried out spoof attacks on either side of the main track, with Window attacks and actually dropping TI's on probable targets along the route. In the case of Nuremberg however PFF's planned route was rejected by the group commanders, and one, single-leg inserted of some 250 miles. Willi Herget, a Luftwaffe night fighter 'ace' with 74 confirmed kills, told me that halfway along this track it was easy to guess at the target, because a line of burning bombers pointed the way to Nuremberg. This disaster was written off as an 'accident', 'one-of-those-things' – but Nuremberg was no accident. It was caused. Oddly enough, to the best of my belief, the PFF routing was never challenged thereafter.

Possibly the greatest compliment that could be paid to the PFF was the manner in which,

towards the end of the war, Bomber Command groups did their own form of path finding, using basic PFF techniques, plus OBOE and GEE-H, the main agents for precision bombing marking. It has been said that this free-for-all, do-it-yourself path finding justified the view that it was wrong to form a corps d'elite, but such a misguided view does not take into account the 'fusing' of the many experienced crews that formed and served in the force, the pooling of operational 'gen', the expertise that developed, the hard-won tactical procedure, and by no means least, the steady improvement in devices provided by the boffins. And finally the determination of the crews to influence a greater weight of bombs to be left in Germany where it hurt most.

The main architect of this incredible advance in bombing efficiency was unquestionably Don Bennett. His single-minded pursuit of operational efficiency had to be witnessed to be really appreciated. He was the only 'operational' group commander in Bomber Command, and he changed the whole concept of strategic bombing. At any one time during his appointment as Air Officer Commanding No 8 Group (PFF), he mustered more flying experience than the sum total of all his contemporary group commanders. Yet strangely, he was the only group commander who served a full tour as an AOC who was not knighted . . . but perhaps that could be another story . . .

Below: EARLY PROBLEMS – Salvo of 500lb HE bombs just after release, demonstrating how they 'tumbled', and thus spoiled accurate trajectories; a factor which led to inaccurate bombing.

Right: BOMBER'S VIEW – Hanover on the night of October 22nd, 1943, so well illuminated by incendiaries that the Salle Strasse shows up as clearly as if on a map. /*Imperial War Museum*

Below right: BOMBS GONE – a stick of 1,000lb MC HE bombs start the plunge towards their target, Mont Candon, on July 19th, 1944, from Lancaster Z-Zebra of 582 Squadron, piloted by Sqn Ldr Sooby, flying at 15,000 ft.

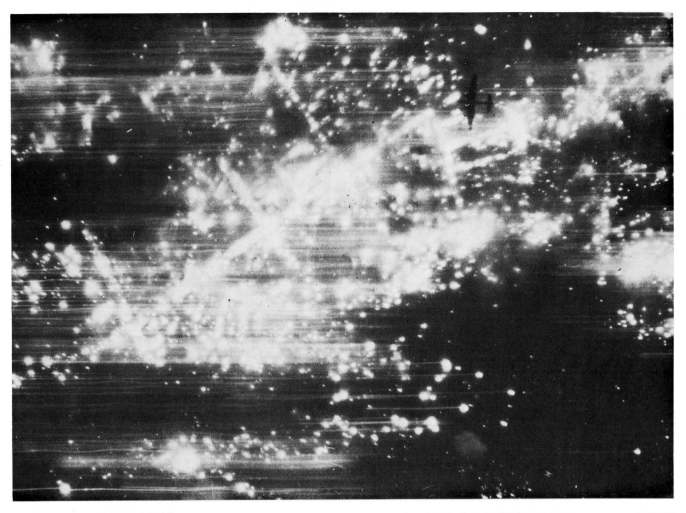

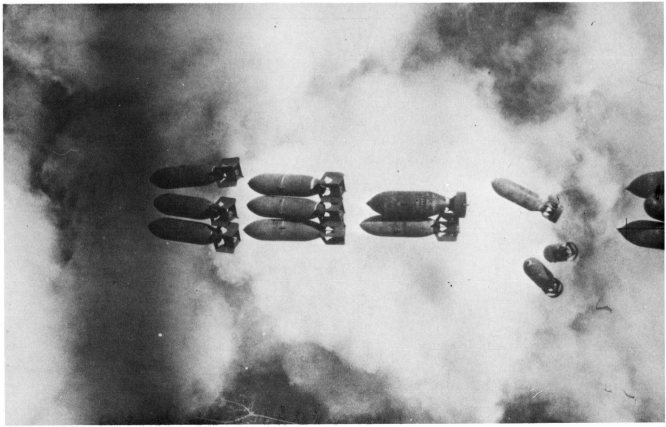

OBOE

FULL REVS – a Mosquito of
the LNSF gives its engines a
final power run at dispersal,
prior to taxying out for a
sortie. In right foreground is
the arm of the groundcrew
erk, holding a torch, ready
to marshal the aircraft onto
the perimeter track.

The full history of the creation, development and eventual operational use of the OBOE device remains to be told; although a wide selection of official and individual accounts of segments of that story have been published over the past 30 years. In the Bomber Command context, one man – perhaps more than any other – has come to be recognised as the leading exponent of OBOE's operational genesis; Group Captain H E Bufton, DSO, OBE, DFC, AFC – 'Hal' to his intimates. Starting in the bleak days of mid-1940, Hal Bufton – then a Flight Lieutenant – was serving as a member of the Blind Approach Technical and Development Unit (BAT & DU) at Boscombe Down; a ponderous title for a small band of dedicated crews investigating means and methods of thwarting the latest Luftwaffe radio beam aids to bombing, *Knickebein*, and, hopefully, searching for some means of exploiting the new radar (then known as Radio Direction Finding or RDF) for possible offensive use in night fighting and, even more remotely, future bombing of Germany. From those early, stumbling days until the end of the war, Hal Bufton was primarily concerned in testing and proving operationally a variety of radar 'black boxes', particularly, after August 1942, with the PFF.

Put in its simplest form, OBOE was a combination of radar pulse signals from two UK stations and basic geometry. By using the known distance to any selected target in Germany as the radii of two separate arcs of a circle; each measured independently from each station, with one station acting as a constant tracking of the bomber; the intersection of the two arcs became the accurate bombing release point. At briefing the bomber crew were given the target and a longitude and latitude point ten minutes flying time from the target; this point being known as the 'Switching on' point. Crews were given a time to be at this point, and began a listening watch some five minutes before it. Each aircraft had a two-letter code and, once this was heard, the transmitter was switched on. The form then took an imaginary beam running from the switch-on point to the target; location of the aircraft at this time – in relation to the 'beam' – being indicated to the pilot by whether he heard dots or dashes (left or right of the beam). On-beam was indicated by a steady note in his ear. Exact position was not known until the crew heard the first letter on the beam; thus with the switch-on point as letter 'D', then a quarter of the way to target was 'C'; half-way, 'B' was given; three quarters of the way, 'A'. It was therefore essential that the aircraft position was never nearer than point 'C' when initially switched-on, otherwise the pilot had no time to get settled on the beam. Once settled, a set airspeed of 260 knots, and a set height 28,000 feet, *had* to be maintained. The release-bombs point was signified after the pilot received point 'A' by listening to the steady note and releasing his load when this cut. Once TI's were dropped it was of prime

Group Captain H E 'Hal' Bufton, DSO, OBE, DFC, AFC, whose pioneer work with a variety of scientific devices, particularly OBOE, with 109 Squadron, was prodigious. Tragically, Hal died in September 1972.
/Imperial War Museum

36

importance to switch off the transmitter to avoid blanketing the ground station, and thereby preventing it calling in the following marker aircraft.

'OBOE was developed as an idea by A H Reeves, his assistant F E Jones, and the rest of his team during 1941, and became hardware by early 1942. This was tested in Wellingtons of 109 Squadron without, at first, any really concrete ideas on how it would be employed. We anticipated that it would be used by individual aircraft to drop bombs accurately, and naturally our thoughts were to have as big an aeroplane as possible which could drop a big load.

The early days of OBOE are closely linked with the German blind bombing systems which came into use in 1940. First of all there was *Knickebein*, which was a fairly crude system which all their aircraft carried; this was jammed fairly easily by the late summer of 1940. The next system was *River* – a system of seven beams used by KG 100, the German Path Finder Group, during late summer and autumn of 1940. I was with the Wireless Intelligence Investigation Unit investigating this system, and we were working closely with Farnborough and the Telecommunications Research Establishment (TRE) at Worth Matravers. We tried to cope with the beams by jamming them and bombing them. In the short term jamming won out and KG 100 had only limited success as Path Finders, including Coventry. While we were

actively bombing the transmitters we ran down the German beams and used either the cone of silence or coast line to judge the bomb release point. However, Farnborough and TRE were both developing devices to help us to bomb and these turned up during the summer of 1941. There was the 'Bailie Beam' which was developed by George Bailie of Farnborough and was very similar to the German *Knickebein*. TRE modified a CHL station and a fighter IFF to give us a bomb release point. Both of these devices came out too late to use against the *River* system, but were used very successfully from about October 1941 to January 1942 against the *Scharnhorst* and *Gneisenau* in Brest. Our 109 Squadron pilots flew Stirlings of 7 and 15 Squadrons which were equipped with a Bailie Beam and the TRE bomb release 'mouse'. I was away at this time, so was not able to take part in this series of trips – the whole operation being known as *Trinity* – but Slim Somerville (Group Captain K J Somerville, DSO, DFC, AFC) played a big part, also Roger Reese. The *Trinity* operations caused at least about six direct hits on the ships and the lock gates, and forced them to make their 'celebrated' dash up the Channel later.

While developing their release device TRE also had a number of ideas on developing a full blind bombing aid. One of the first ideas was an 'H' system, which was later developed into GEE-H; an alternative plot was developed as OBOE. During the very early work on

GRIM REAPER – the grisly insigne on the nose of Mosquito B.IV, DK333 of 109 Squadron. Coded HS-F, its bomb log shows 29 completed operational sorties, and was originally the aircraft usually flown by Wg Cdr K J 'Slim' Somerville, DSO, DFC, AFC./*Wg Cdr F Ruskell*, DFC

OBOE I was involved by attending a session at TRE (called a 'Sunday Soviet') at which Air Marshal Joubert agreed that my unit (WIDU, later 109 Squadron) should do the development flying rather than TRE's own flying unit. Actually Joubert's job then gave him no right to make this decision – however, it stuck. We did early trials of the bombing release device during 1941 and a tracking aid called a 'Howler Chaser'. This was a crazy device (which meant something on the ground but nothing in the air), by which you were meant to hold your track by keeping the signal at a low audio frequency. If you moved to either side the pitch increased and became a howl when you were way off track. Since the pitch increased whether you went left or right, it was impossible to use in the air, but it gave the radar experts all the answers they needed for later development. We had a young laboratory technician who flew with us called Bates. He was a keen musician and said that the device sounded like an oboe – which is where the name came from.

Sometime in 1941 the OBOE project was taken over by Reeves' team; a large one which included Dr F E Jones as 'head boy', and Dr C L Smith, B Blanchard and Hooper. This team developed its ideas very quickly and I remember a hot day in the early summer of 1941 at Worth Matravers when Reeves and Jones took time out to explain as much of their system to me as I could understand. I think they took our advice on one point and used the same presentation to the air crew as the Germans used in their *River* system; that is, a fairly high pitched note of about 2,000 c/s and a beam speed of about 120 dots a minute. When I came back to 109 Squadron in early 1942, *Trinity* operations were finished and my flight concentrated on the development of OBOE. Another flight of 109, under Vic Willis, was investigating the German night fighter radar and were 'lucky' enough on several occasions to get intercepted – with fairly disastrous results! They succeeded, however, in getting the necessary information on German A.I. and, later, this flight developed into the radio counter-measures half of 100 Group. The third flight of 109 continued to monitor the German beams, and was run by George Grant who joined PFF early in 1943 as a flight commander on 156 Squadron at Warboys, and was station commander at Little Staughton in 1944 when 109 moved there.

The full OBOE concept was that there could be up to 20 aircraft operating together on the same radio frequency channel, by using different pulse recurrence frequencies. In the event the capabilities of using this number of aircraft did not materialise until the final form of OBOE, Mk III, came in at the end of the war.

In the Mark I and Mark II versions we were limited to one aircraft on each RF channel, so that we could only operate two aircraft at a time with Mark I which only had two channels. Even Mark III, in its initial form in 1945, could only work one aircraft at a time. The original OBOE trials were done using Mark I (on 200 m/cs). It was known that this frequency band would not give us operational security from jamming, and it was first expected that we would have to wait for the 10 centimetre Mark II sets before we could begin actual operations. Since Mark I was working by mid-1942, it was decided that it would be used on operations even with its limitation of only two channels and the probability that it would be jammed within a few months.

By early 1942 OBOE was becoming practicable, it was decided that the only suitable aeroplane for it was the Wellington VI. This was one of the really tremendous aircraft of the war, but unfortunately never had the chance to prove itself in anger. It had a seven pound pressure cabin, and a cruising speed of 280mph at 35,000-plus feet; its 4,000 lb bomb load was felt acceptable because OBOE would put it in the right place. We had tried hard to persuade ourselves that the Lancaster could do the job, but with its relatively low

Above left: CAMOUFLAGE PATTERNS – Mosquito YH-S of 21 Squadron, viewed from 20,000 ft by Mosquito B-Baker of 109 Sqn, on April 28th, 1944, en route to an unspecified target. An interesting illustration of how an aircraft's camouflage pattern could 'merge' into the earth below.

Left: ML963, 8K-K, a Mosquito B.XVI of 571 Squadron, LNSF, which was based at Oakington in late 1944. This particular aircraft had been modified with an enlarged bomb bay to accommodate a 4,000lb High Capacity (HC) 'Cookie' blast bomb internally./*Charles E Brown*

Above: Group Captain George Grant, DSO, DFC, who commanded 109 Squadron and later, RAF Graveley.

Above: **Wing Commander John Northrop, DSO, DFC, AFC**, who served with 100 Group; commanded 83 and 692 Squadrons, PFF. Like 'Hamish' Mahaddie and John Searby, Northrop started his RAF career as an aircraft apprentice at Halton, Buckinghamshire./ *Imperial War Museum*

Above right: TOP DOG – **Mosquito LR503, GB-F of 105 Squadron** which completed a war total of 213 operational sorties – a record for any individual aircraft.

Right: POT-BELLY – a **Mosquito B.XVI** modified to accommodate a 4,000lb HC 'Cookie' bomb in its bomb bay./*De Havilland Aircraft Co.*

ceiling we could not count on it operating higher than 24,000 feet, which would have been useless. (We thought of using the Mosquito early in 1942 but its – then – small 2,000 lb bomb load precluded it). The blind bombing trials which we had done in 1941 were from Wellingtons on the range at Stormy Down, Porthcawl. From memory, out of some 150-plus practice bombs dropped blind from 10,000 feet, we got an average error of 108 yards. Later on, in trials done in 1945 from Mosquitos, the results were about 80 yards from 30,000 feet. In the Wellington VI we used to fly in shirtsleeves with no oxygen at 30,000 feet in perfect comfort, apart from the fear that the pressure cabin was going to burst at any minute. Having settled our choice of the Wellington VI we took delivery of three or four of them, and a modification programme was undertaken by the Ministry of Aircraft Production (MAP) to fit 60 of them with OBOE, and modify them in several ways; in particular, to fit an emergency exit! The only method of getting out of a standard production model was to unscrew the pressure cabin floor, which took about half a minute, and then walk 40 feet down the fuselage to the rear exit.

Meanwhile, having noted the relative effectiveness of the German target finders,

KG 100, from late 1940; the idea of a target finding force was being pushed by Air Ministry against Bomber Command resistance, and by mid-1942 the principle of establishing such a force in Bomber Command had been forced through. First ideas were that the 'target finders' would include an illuminating-flare force, followed by a specially experienced group which would mark the target visually with large 'splashers' of incendiaries. However, at just about this time Dr Coxen of the MAP came up with what was, for those days, the perfect target marking device. (To my personal disgruntlement, the armament experts having said that an effective marker was virtually impossible when we presented them with the problem in 1940 . . .) Coxen's idea was to put 60 large 'candles', made of Very Light cartridge material, in a canister, fitted with a barometric fuze, which would explode the canister and ignite the 'candles' at a predetermined height. Initially this was 3,000 feet but later on was reduced. When exploded at 3,000 feet the target indicator (TI) bloomed into a magnificent splurge of colour – red, green and yellow – which slowly drifted to the ground and stayed burning for about three minutes in all. Now all the bits came together – there was the principle of a target-finding force, Coxen's TI, Reeves' OBOE, and the Mosquito. With the need for a large bomb capacity now unnecessary, the Mosquito became the natural aircraft for us. And it was 109's commanding officer, Wing Commander C C McMullin, who was the man who produced the last gleam of genius to put the bits together – one week before the final decision to begin installation of the Wellington VI on a production basis he got hold of a Mosquito and installed all our bits in it, just in time for the conference. The Wellington was rejected in favour of the Mosquito.

We did the very first OBOE operation with Mosquito IV's on December 20th, 1942, against a coking plant at Lutterade, in east Holland. Our operational strength then was six crews and eight aircraft. Six went to Lutterade, which was supposed to be a clean target, bereft of bomb holes, and therefore one we could use as a calibration objective to check OBOE accuracy. In fact it proved useless for this purpose; photographs later showed that the target was smothered with bombs from some earlier attack. Four more 109 crews were trained by January 1943, and by June we had about 20 crews. In July 1943, 105 Squadron was linked with 109 as the second OBOE squadron; some of their crews being trained for OBOE, and the rest going to 139 Squadron to become the first of the Mosquito Light Night Bombing Force (LNBF).

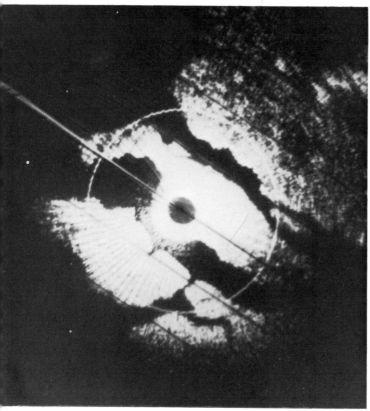

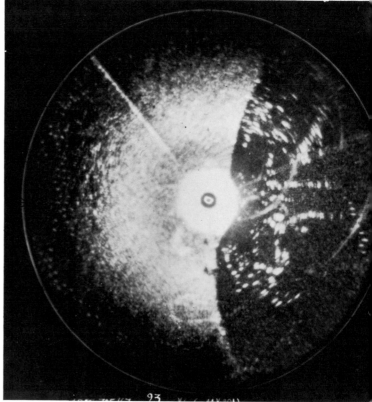

Above left: HOT SEAT – a 4,000lb HC bomb, trollied for loading into Mosquito DZ637, a B.IV Series II of 692 Sqn at Graveley, early 1944. The non-aircrew officer is Wing Commander W J R Shepherd, OBE, No 8 Group's Intelligence Officer/*Hawker-Siddeley Aviation*

Far left: Typical H2S 'pictures' – the first showing Flakkee and Rotterdam from 16,000 ft on the night of 20th/21st December, 1943, as seen from Lancaster G-George, 83 Squadron; whilst the second view shows the Allied invasion fleet just off the Normandy coast on June 6th, 1944.

Above: MARKER MOSSIE – Mosquito about to receive its quota of 250lb Target Indicators (TI's), Yellow. Hooked on and released like a normal HE store, the TI's were a significant aid to precision./*Flight International*

Left: GOING DOWN – a 1,000lb MC HE bomb, filled with Minol 2 explosive, dropping onto Calais on September 25th, 1944, from Lancaster 'G' of 635 Squadron (Sqn Ldr Henderson), from 6,000 ft. The compact, shorter tail unit fitted here permitted greater overall tonnage to be carried per aircraft.

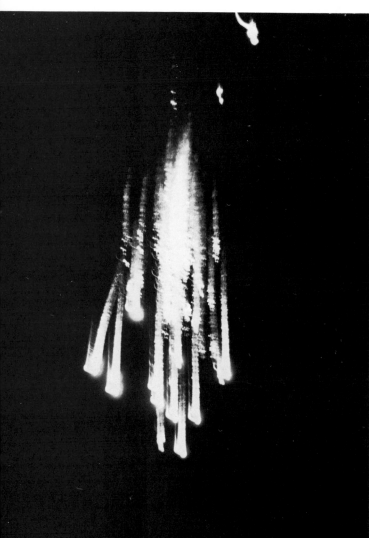

Above left: SKY-MARKING.
Four green TI's plunging
into cloud over Berlin on
November 23rd/24th, 1943.
from Lancaster O of 156
Squadron at 18,000 ft.
Skipper of O-Orange was
Pilot Officer M C Stimpson
(later Flt Lt, DFC), who was
killed on February 15th, 1944
over Germany.

Above: Graphic illustration
of the efficiency of a TI
marker; photo taken on the
night of February 26th, 1944.

Left: CHRISTMAS TREE –
the nickname applied by the
Germans to the PFF's

colourful pyrotechnic target
markers; and well
demonstrated by this
German photo of a TI
bursting./*Bundesarchiv*

Above right: FLARES – a
quartet of 4-inch flares
stowed near their chute in a
Short Stirling. In each flare's
nose can be seen the
barometric fuse which
ignited the pyrotechnic at a
pre-determined height above
the target./*Flight International*

Right: ROLLING – an
LNSF Mosquito starts its
take-off run at full power.
/*Imperial War Museum*

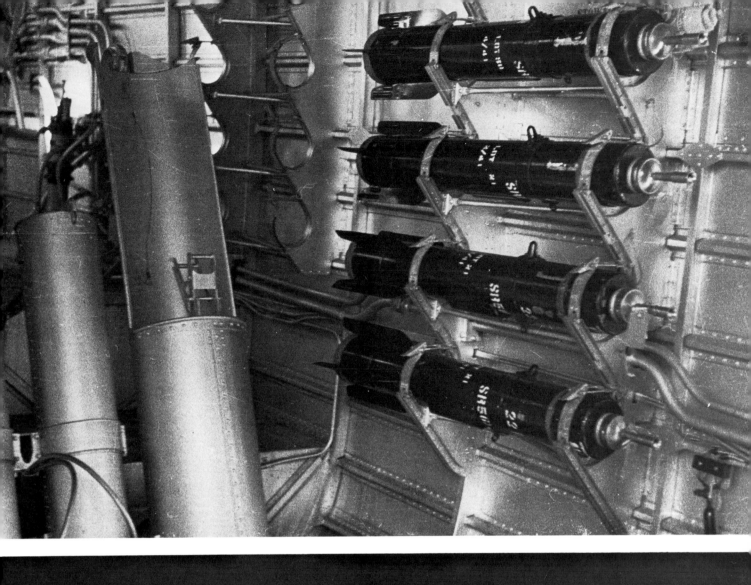

Ops Tonight

'Andy' was a navigator, yet in many ways the antithesis of the popular image of an operational bomber crew member. A schoolmaster in peacetime, he joined the RAF in 1940 as a lowly Pilot Officer in administration. The death of an air crew friend led him to volunteer for flying and, despite 'advancing age' and a suspect right eye, he managed to pass on to training in Canada, and then onto bomber operations. He soon discovered another inherent 'weakness' – he was air-sick every time he flew. That he overcame all obstacles and continued on operations is evidenced by the fact that he left the Royal Air Force in 1954 as Wing Commander E W Anderson, OBE, DFC, AFC. His connections with the PFF

go back to its origin, when he joined Don Bennett as the senior navigation officer on the headquarters staff. He remained with the force for two years; often going on operations to test new ideas and gadgets. Modest and self-effacing by nature, yet his navigation logs were later used by post-war bomber crew instructors as model examples; 'Andy' Anderson represents the many men who went to war 'reluctantly' but from a strong sense of simple duty.

The most striking thing about operations is the unreality. You wake up in the morning, warm, safe, and comfortable, roll out of bed, wash, shave, and stroll through the fields to

the mess for breakfast. The sun is shining and the little white clouds are chasing each other across the sky. Everything is quiet and peaceful. Only – curious thought – you may be shot at tonight.

At about 10 o'clock the word comes round, 'Ops tonight, briefing at 1800 – six o'clock'. The routine work goes on, a training flight with a new navigator, a visit to the gen-men who look after the 'magic eye' on the aircraft to discuss a mysterious fault that developed the night before last; or a browse in the intelligence library reading reports of past raids and looking at photographs of the results.

The navigators' briefing begins half an hour earlier than the main briefing. The room is a long, low Nissen hut with 15 or 20 tables and a 100 or so chairs all facing an array of maps and blackboards. There is a large wall map of Europe covered with red and blue patches to show the Hun defences. The route is marked out with coloured tape, and by the target a collection of brightly-coloured pins indicate the colours of the markers that will be dropped. On the blackboard to one side is a large drawing of the target; on the other side is another blackboard with a list of skippers who are 'on', together with times of

take-off, bomb loads, and so on. Above is a third blackboard, long and thin, with a cross-section of the weather and the clouds to be expected on the journey.

Out of the satchel comes the chart – pink. The route to be followed must first be drawn, and then a flight plan calculated. This is a forecast for the flight, complete with the times for the various stages or 'legs', and the directions in which the aircraft must be flown to offset the drifting caused by the wind. The work is done very carefully and precisely, and the mind escapes gratefully into a maze of intricate little niceties. The height that we shall cross the enemy coast is at the moment just an academic problem.

The rest of the crew come in and chatter and are helpful and distracting, but by six o'clock the work is nearly finished. Then the squadron commander walks over towards the map of Europe, and the talking dies away as we settle back in our chairs to listen. Even the briefing itself is curiously remote and unreal, full of drab technicalities. First, weather; cloud heights, freezing levels, icing indexes – 'moderate icing in the layers of strato-cumulus cloud.' Then the route; 'turning point, 52.17 north, zero zero west, then on a track of one-four-two true . . .' – we note it all

NIGHT RUN. A Lancaster B.III about to roll on the night of February 16th, 1944./*Imperial War Museum*

down. Next, the exact instructions for the target; 'If there's more than seven-tenths of cloud below, primary flare-droppers will revert to the role of blind markers dropping sky-markers yellow with green stars' – and so on. The details of the run-in; '. . . come in at 17,000, air speed 170 indicated, release first bundle 27 seconds after coincidence' – cold, impartial, and precise. England expects that every man will have his stop-watch working accurately. One last word, 'There's four pounds eleven on it tonight, and the photos before zero don't count.' For we each put a shilling into the pool every trip, and the crew that gets the best aiming point photo, scoops the lot. And we turn and grin at the crew who were disqualified for cheating the other night. On the last operation that crew had deliberately gone into the target two minutes early, all alone with no protection, just to get a picture before the smoke of battle spoilt it – the cads!

Briefing is over. The gunners, wireless operators and flight engineers drift away, and the pilots, navigators and bomb aimers are left to make the final arrangements and to complete the flight plan. Soon everything is ready, and we go down to the Mess for supper. The operational 'supper' is a curious business. For some extraordinary reason it must consist of bacon and eggs, which is just about the worst thing possible on which to fly. For the fried food makes gas inside, and as you fly up into the rarer air four miles up, you swell a little and feel the more uncomfortable. Yet cries of rage and disappointment would rend the air if for this traditional dish a more digestible titbit was substituted. So we eat our bacon and eggs and think how lucky we are and how the poor types in civvy street must envy us with their one or two eggs a month. Afterwards, we sip our coffee and then the word comes round that transport has arrived to carry us up to the airfield.

From now until we are off the ground the tension will grow. The mind slips away to a safe distance, and sits somewhere far off, watching the hands pull on flying boots and tie the knots on the tapes of the Mae West. It listens, detached, to the last instructions from the skipper. Suddenly stops and catches itself in the curious feeling that exactly this has happened somewhere before. Looks at the sunset and counts the rooks going home, and then contemplates the body climbing into the lorry. Is suddenly grateful for the cheerfulness of the gunner sitting on the tailboard. Climbs into the aircraft and watches while the chart is pinned down. Smiles ironically at the grin and the thumbs-up sign that you give the skipper as he clambers by, and notices how effeminate he looks in his helmet, like a bathing cap. Then sits and waits. Knowing that in three hours' time the body will be over

MOTHERS MEETING – AVM Don Bennett chairs the morning meeting in the Operations Room of PFF headquarters, Wyton, to decide details of that night's raids. From left (facing): Wg Cdr 'Mickey' Finn, senior OBOE controller; John Jukes, Operational Research; Wing Commander M J Thomas, B Sc, Group Meteorological Officer; Don Bennett; Group Captain C D C Boyce, SASO; Squadron Leader W Rathbone, Group Armament Officer. Back to camera is the duty navigation officer (at wall map) and duty operations officer, both unidentifiable.

the target. And that once there, some twisted pride will drive it to do the job almost against the will of the mind itself.

Then comes loneliness and a longing for the waiting to be over. The operation, that will be a cold impersonal routine once it has begun, seems awful as the huge, black shapes of childhood's dreams. A message. 'Operations scrubbed. Weather over target is hopeless.' Flat, cold and deflated, like the shrivelled toy balloons of yesterday's Christmas party, we climb heavily out of the aircraft and go back to the changing room, the mess, and to bed. Safe, warm, comfortable again. Only – there will be tomorrow night.

Climax

'Oxygen full on'. In six minutes' time we shall be over Berlin amongst the first wave of Path Finders. But our 'magic eye' has broken down, and so I am lying down in the bomb-aimer's position glaring through a sheet of glass at the ground four miles below. We shall not drop our fireworks, for eyes are liable to mislead, wishful seeing is all too easy, and there are only two places for our markers, the exact aiming point or the bomb bays. Yet our journey will not have been wasted. We shall go in with the first wave and that will help to swamp the defences. If we do get 'picked on', well, someone else will get a free run-in. And, incidentally, we have in addition to our mark-ers several tons of bombs on board which will do the target just a little bit of no good. So at the moment we are all eyes and perhaps that little extra oxygen may help. For we must find out where we are so that we don't blunder along all on our own.

The defences are waking up. Ahead, slightly to port, are great, menacing cones of searchlights that divide and come together and divide again, like sinister but stately folk dancers. Flashes of light in the sky are appearing to starboard, flak bursts, looking somehow surprised like asterisks. 'Three minutes to go' from the navigator. 'Can you see anything?' from the skipper. 'Searchlight coming up behind to port' from the tail gunner, and one of the points of light at the bottom of a pale beam becomes dazzling and lights up the bomb sight and the frost on the window, and then fades and passes on. No sign yet of the early flare-droppers. They ought to be on target by now. And in spite of the voice of past experience, the present doubt comes stealing in, are we alone? Are the others with us? Why is everything so horribly quiet?

Quite gently, a little ball of golden light appears far below and to starboard, and then another and another. Beside them little patches of houses begin to grow, and reflections of water and roads. The first Path Finder flares are down. More golden balls appear, silently and mysteriously, and these little

A night's operations, marked on the HQ PFF Operations Room wall map, showing a typical routing plan, including markers, bombers, spoof sorties et al. This specific map was for the night of Saturday, October 14th, 1944, when targets included Berlin, Duisburg, Ludwigshaven, Hamburg and Dusseldorf.

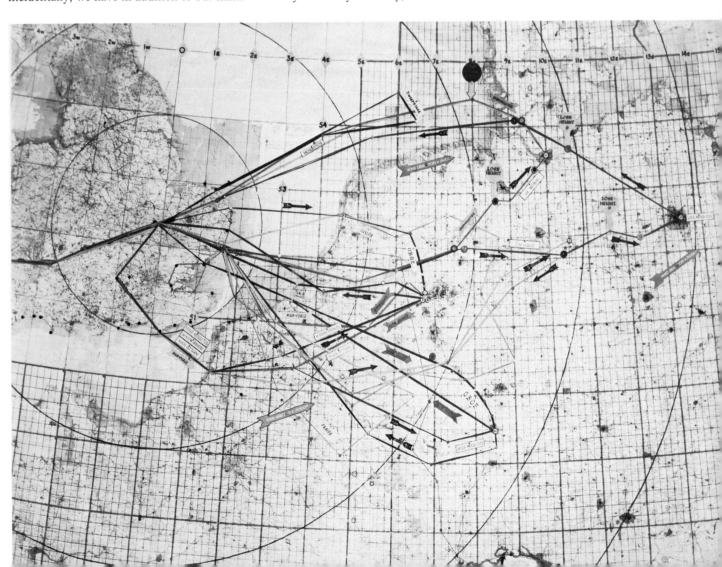

patches piece slowly together. Quite suddenly, there is that bend of the river, there the railway station, there the great wide avenues run together, there is the Templehof! Berlin is spread out ahead and to starboard. The skipper swings the aircraft over and I am pressed hard down onto the floor. Slowly, very slowly, the world tilts, and the lights of those flares swing round ahead. Then we level out for the final bombing run. Time stands still. The target lies quietly before us with the little golden balls floating just above it. More searchlights spring into life and flashes appear on the ground, either guns or bombs from the flare-dropping Path Finders. A bump tells us that we have flown through a slip-stream. Ahead and below the black shape of a Lancaster, tilted slightly, slides across in front and disappears to port. Puffs of smoke, black against the searchlights below, run by. Then just ahead a little worm of pale green fire appears abruptly in the sky and sprays forward like shining drops of water from the rose of a watering can, then splashes suddenly alongside the railway station. 'Bomb doors open'.

After that there is nothing but those green markers and the cross of light on the bomb-sight, like the handle of a sword. Those bright flashes are photographs being taken, those big, dull, slow splashes of light are 'cookies' those quick spurts are guns firing or 500-pounders bursting. Two more green markers go down

and make a rough triangle, and then right in the middle falls a red so that the aim is shifted a little. For tonight, specially picked crews are carrying red markers which will be dropped only if they are absolutely sure of their aim. Very slowly the red marker creeps up underneath the aircraft. The whole world is concentrated in your two eyes. A word and the markers are twitched a little to the right, and now they are just touching the sword blade itself. There is no Berlin, there is no bomber, just a red mark and a sword handle. Slowly the mark slides up the hilt, and for a second the sword handle is poised above it, and then with all my might I squeeze the tit, my right thumb forcing the button down into its socket, as I drive those bombs out of the bomb bays down onto the target below. 'Bombs going' – the little light by the bomb switches goes out – 'Bombs gone'. I peer forward and watch them go, black and shiny in the searchlights.

It is hopeless to try to tell where those bombs actually hit. Sticks are dancing continuously across the target. Deep, angry, red pools are lighting up below the smoke. Intense white flashes and slower yellow gleams, waving searchlights and red flak bursts. The navigator's voice comes over the intercomm, 'Course out two-nine-one, two-nine-one', and I realise that I am still squeezing the bomb tit desperately. I climb up and stand beside the pilot. Slowly, so slowly, the

Below: INTRUDERS – just some of the Mosquito fighters' crews who flanked the main bomber streams, raiding singly against Luftwaffe aerodromes to obviate some of the German opposition. 418 Sqn navigators checking maps are, left to right: Fg Offs L Abelson; H A Hague; A J Brown; J D Armstrong; Flt Sgts H Williams and H Gurnett – seen here at Ford airfield. All were Canadians except Williams, who came from London.
/*Keystone Press Agency*

Right: CLIMBING INTO THE CLOBBER – bomber crews kitting up in their flying clothing prior to a raid. Inner excitement, at this stage, was steadily mounting; exemplified by the many cigarettes, last-minute jokes . . ./*Pictorial Press*

Below right: CHECK OXYGEN – a Lancaster crew tests its oxygen masks for serviceability before leaving.
/*Pictorial Press*

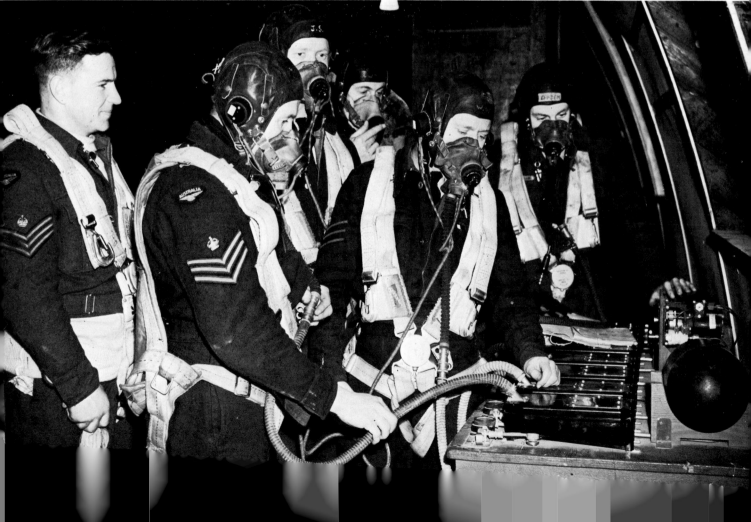

aircraft banks over and dips one wing into the smoke and fire that is Berlin. Suddenly a red dotted line of tracer shells goes streaming by our wing tip, not aimed at us, but there must be fighters about. Over the target something is burning in the sky, an aircraft is on fire, and the green lights are falling from it. She blows up with a slow red flash and pieces go flaming down while the searchlights hold for a few moments onto the cloud of black smoke.

The aircraft levels off and we set out on our long struggle home. Flying blindly on calculations, helped a little by the line of searchlights by Magdeburg, and the cones at Bremen and Wilhelmshaven, we cross the German coast at last and head out across the North Sea for England and bacon and eggs. Soon the searchlights are left behind, and everything seems quiet and still. Then, far below on the water, a little light starts blinking faintly. And the mind sees three or four men huddled in a dinghy, cold and wet. There is just nothing we can do. We circle once and then carry on. When we get back we shall be able to estimate the position and let the rescue boys know. So we leave the little light winking desperately behind until finally it is lost to sight. And we are silent for a little while.

The ring of lights round base twinkle cheerfully up at us and we learn that our 'turn to land is number three. Fly at 4,000 feet.' Then follows a code word to tell us that there are no intruders about. Intruders are Hun night fighters who sneak across with the returning bombers hoping to shoot them down as they come in to land. We circle the airfield, seeing every now and then the green and red wing-tip lights of other aircraft stooging round waiting their turn to land. Below is the flarepath, a double row of lights, with a red and green pin-prick crawling along between them as a Lancaster lands on the runway.

A few minutes later and we are bumping along between those two rows of lights, and taxying round to Dispersal between lines of faint blue glow-worms, waved on by ground crew with torches. 'Are they all back?' is the first question. 'All but one have either landed or are overhead.' An hour later and the interrogation is over. 'Any news?' 'Still one not back yet.' And we remember the aircraft that blew up over the target, and the light on the water that we left winking behind us. We go back to the mess for food. And afterwards, 'Any news?' 'Afraid not'. In a few day's time seven new faces will be on the squadron – that's all . . .

Left: **Whilst the air crews are being briefed, the ground crews have been at full stretch preparing the aircraft for operations. Hundreds of details to check scrupulously, then test and re-test. Here, two engine mechanics listen critically to a Halifax's Merlins during the pre-flight inspection.** | *Imperial War Museum*

Above: **In the bomb dump. Armourers of a Halifax unit start loading bomb trollies with canisters of 4lb incendiaries during the winter 1944-45.**/*Imperial War Museum*

Left: On a Lancaster unit, other armourers are loading 4lb incendiaries into SBC's (Small Bomb Containers). /*Imperial War Museum*

Below: WOMEN'S LIB – 1943 style. A cheerful WAAF at the helm of a bomb 'train', ready to deliver to the dispersal.

Right: WHEEL 'EM IN – Halifax Q-Queenie of 405 Squadron RCAF ready for its bomb load. The job called for raw muscle-power as the 'plumbers' heave a trolley of 1,000lb HE bombs round into alignment with the bomb bay; whilst, at right, an erk puts the finishing touches to the SBC's./*Imperial War Museum*

Below right: Once under the bomb bay, each bomb is hoisted up to its bomb station. At the same time the inboard wing racks of Halifax Q-Queenie receive their load of SBC's, in this case, filled with 30lb J incendiary bombs./*Imperial War Museum*

Left: LANCASTER LOAD – a clutch of 1,000lb MC HE bombs about to be 'digested' by the capacious bomb bay of a Lanc. Chalk markings on the bomb noses, 'Fuzed 43', indicate that No 43 air-armed nose pistols have been fitted in the bombs. Safety pins – still fitted to the pistols here – will be removed only when the air crew is ready to climb in finally. Scene on March 22nd, 1944, prior to a raid on Frankfurt./*Imperial War Museum*

Below left: A NIGHT'S RATIONS – Lancaster awaiting its load of 1,000lb and 500lb HE bombs. These are tail-fused only, indicating a delayed-action load.

Below: NOT-SO-LIGHT BOMBER – Mosquito DZ637 of 692 Squadron at Graveley, about to be loaded with a 4,000lb HC HE bomb; a weight slightly heavier than the early American B-17 'Flying Fortress' carried . . .!
/*Keystone Agency*

Bottom: THEIR MORALE WAS ALWAYS HIGH – the bomber crews climb aboard transport, bound for their aircraft at dispersal; to the ribald accompaniment of remarks and gestures from another waiting crew.

Top left: ALL OFF – debussing (in the RAF phrase . . .) at dispersal.

Centre left: Checking the rations before climbing in

Right: THE OFFICE. Cockpit and pilot's dashboard, in a Halifax B.II. In bottom right corner can just be seen the access to the bomb aimer's nose position./*Flight International*

Below: TAXI RANK. Scene at Scampton in 1942 as Lancasters of 83 Squadron stream towards the run-way for take-off; a scene typical of the main force bomber stations prior to any raid. /*Imperial War Museum*

Top: GETTING THE GREEN. Lancaster of 83 Squadron receives the green light 'GO' signal from a hand-operated signal lamp, and prepares to take off.

Above: THE 'OFF' – with a last wave from some WAAFs gathered at the end of the runway.

Left: FIRST LEG – Lancasters settle at low height and head out towards the North Sea.

Above right: EN ROUTE – Lancasters of 405 Squadron RCAF, PFF drone towards Germany; nearest aircraft being LQ-U-Uncle.

Right: PILOT'S PANORAMA – cloudscape viewed from the pilot's seat of a 1409 Flight Mosquito at 29,000 ft, on September 26th, 1943.

Left: MIXED LOAD. 1,000lb HE and 500lb Cluster bombs dropping on Osnabruck from Lancaster T-Tommie, 635 Squadron (Sqn Ldr Mange), on March 25th, 1945, from 15,500 ft.

Below left: ILLUMINATION. Target Indicator bursting over the heart of Berlin on the night of April 11/12th, 1945, viewed from a Mosquito ('T') of 139 Squadron, piloted by Flt Lt Alcock, flying at 27,000 ft.

Below: A mixture of TI's and searchlights produced this pattern of illumination over Dusseldorf on September 10/11th, 1942./*Imperial War Museum*

Right: HOME AGAIN – crews enjoy the post-ops 'aircrew' egg, though fatigue and nervous reaction is etched into each man's face.

Below right: RESULTS. Aiming point photos are displayed outside the squadron headquarters, where they can be studied by the ground crews – the end results of the erks' labours. The rearmost erk wears a white 'flash' in his Service cap; indicating that he has been accepted for air crew training.

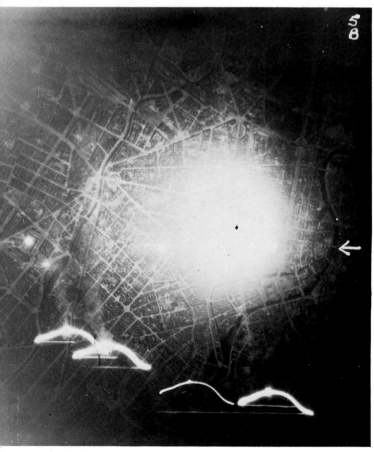

Just a Desk Job

PATH FINDER CREW. A 7 Squadron Lancaster crew at Oakington, including Gordon Graham (2nd from left); 'Lucky' Hudson, Navigator (3rd from left); skipper 'Flash' J McCollah (centre). The bomb log of the Lanc records 80 operations completed.

The first rule of the Path Finder Force was not that you must be clever, nor that you must be brave, but simply that you *must* be reliable. Accuracy in all things and absolutely precise in timing. Hence the onus of final responsibility for the success or failure of any operation weighed heavily on the shoulders of the navigators. On their skill and dedication depended many things – not least the lives of the crews in the following main force bombers. Arrival over a target for the initial marking *had* to be at the appointed time – every other facet of the operation was carefully planned from that focal point. A few minutes late – or early – could mean the difference between success and survival; or disaster in the air. For the majority of navigators each operation was a long grind of sheer work, bent over a navigational table with all the paraphernalia of logs, charts, pencils and instruments; shut off by a small black-out curtain from the rest of the crew, with only intercomm connection to reassure them of the physical presence of the rest of their crew. Indeed, one navigator – a veteran of nearly 70 operations eventually – complained bitterly when, on initial selection for air crew duties, he was refused pilot training and offered only a navigator's job. 'Hell, I joined the RAF to fly and fight against Germany; and all you can offer me is just another bloody desk job!!'. Entirely engrossed with his instruments, a navigator

seldom bothered to even look out of the nearby window at what was going on around him. One who did, after a number of operations over Berlin, was finally persuaded by his skipper to come out of his cubby-hole to see the 'end results'. Taking one look at the holocaust below, bursting flak all round, the navigator croaked, 'My God! – and swiftly disappeared behind his curtain again, never to look outside during the rest of his operational tour.

Gordon Graham was a navigator with the PFF, and flew three tours of operations – a total in his case of 82 ops; all with 7 Squadron. His reminiscences here are fragmentary; merely facets of a much longer story that he – and so many others – could tell.

One did not realise it at the time, indeed I feel it would have invoked a sense of shame to do so, but my 13 months of operations were the most exciting and, indeed, enjoyable period of my life. We arrived on 7 Squadron, based then at Oakington, near Cambridge, immediately following the notorious Nuremberg raid late in March 1944, during which Bomber Command suffered its heaviest losses on one night. And within the period of March 22nd to May 26th, 7 Squadron had four commanding officers; Group Captain K Rampling, DSO, DFC, who was lost on March 22nd; Wing Commander W G Lockhart,

Below: THE LAST MOMENTS – a crew wait by their Lancaster, ready to start another sortie.

Below right: The view from the cockpit of the Foret de Mormal, France, on August 9th, 1944, from 8-10,000 ft. A photo taken from a 35 Squadron Lancaster, piloted by Squadron Leader Alan Craig, DSO, DFC.

DSO, DFC, who died on April 28th; and Wing Commander J F Barron, DSO, DFC, who failed to return on May 20th. Barron was succeeded by Wing Commander R W Cox, DFC, AFC. Since it was the practice of the squadron commander to operate from time to time during his period of office, and some CO's took their respective functional leaders with them as crew, the turnover of senior posts could be fairly rapid. Almost a complete clear-out of 'top' people resulted when Wing Commander Lockhart failed to return, as in his crew he had the squadron navigation officer and at least three other squadron officers of differing functions. Bearing in mind that from October 1942 there had been only two other CO's before Group Captain Rampling, the initial introduction of our crew, skippered by Alan Craig, was therefore a little disconcerting.

We were three weeks after Nuremberg before we visited Germany again. There was then a two-months run-up to the Normandy invasion, so looking back it is now evident that in fact we arrived at just the favourable moment. My first two tours were with Alan Craig and constitute over two-thirds of my flying, and therefore I knew the crew members more intimately. Alan was dedicated, and did everything in the approved manner. Crew discipline was first class, and when odd people stood in for sickness et al, they re-marked on this to others. We went to Stuttgart on the night of July 28th, 1944, in Lancaster U-Uncle, and we had the task of Master of Ceremonies (the title later became Master Bomber). The gunnery leader, Squadron Leader Dixon, stood in for us as rear gunner. He was first class at his job, and flew with us on about six occasions. I had a faith in him just born out of intuition, and from watching the way he went about his job. After being over the target area from beginning to end of the raid, I gave Alan a course for home, and we left as planned. Within 15 minutes, Dickie called up in the approved manner, 'Rear Gunner to Pilot, there's fighters about'. Back came, 'OK Rear Gunner'. Then – 'Rear Gunner to Pilot, fighter starboard quarter, prepare to corkscrew starboard.' Just then the mid-upper gunner said, 'I think he's coming over to port.' Then Dickie called out, 'Starboard, go.' Alan, in his best top drawer voice said, 'Now what do you want? Port or starboard' Back came the prompt reply from Dickie, 'Starboard, you – , down starboard, rolling back up port.' The dull rattle of the Brownings crept over the intercomm. Then the terminating punch-line from Dickie, 'Got the bastard'. Confirmed by the mid-upper gunner. Such was the intercomm discipline that there was no more comment about that fighter, or any related discussion until we reached Oakington.

Below: PATH FINDER. The late Wing Commander Alan J L Craig, DSO, DFC, who served brilliantly with 7 and 35 Squadrons; and after the war commanded 35 Squadron when its Lancasters visited America on a goodwill mission.
/ Imperial War Museum

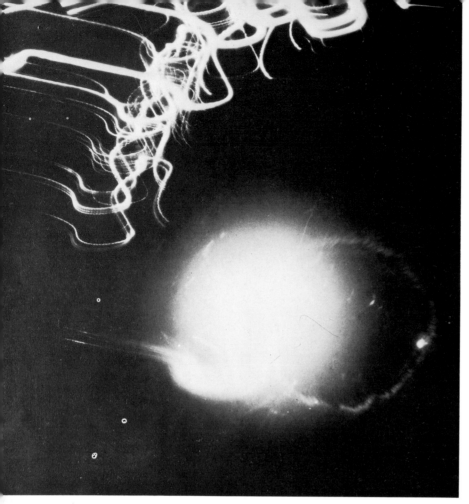

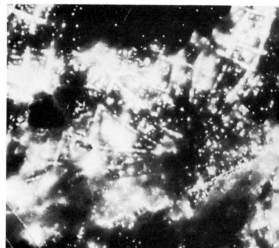

Above: Karlsruhe on the receiving end, as a 4,000lb HC 'Cookie' bomb explodes on the night of 2nd/3rd September, 1942./*Imperial War Museum*

Top right: Munich night scene, December 21st, 1944.

Above right: Munster suburbs ablaze during a devastating fire raid – '. . . all lit up like an illuminated street directory . . .', as one crew member described it afterwards.

I took a great deal of pride in my job as navigator. I suppose to the members of the crew it bordered on conceit. Despite the fact that Alan knew this, and that I had never let him down, he did on three or four occasions irritate me by not offering the blind faith, to which I believed I was entitled. It matters nothing now that on each occasion I was proved right, because he was the best pilot with whom I ever flew. He was tops at his job and I owed it to him to try to emulate him.

Our first step to a leading role on the squadron was on our 14th trip, when we were given the job of deputy Master of Ceremonies to Wing Commander S 'Tubbie' Baker. Tubbie had the most seasoned navigator on the unit, Squadron Leader Doug Brown – alongside Doug's experience I was a mere starter. The route out to target took us over the south coast, south of the Channel Islands, over Brittany and Normandy. It was agreed at briefing that Alan would call up Tubbie at 23.00 over France, to exchange some detail, a brief contact, but to confirm bombing height in code, based on weather observation. After the brief exchange, which because of moonlight and good weather conditions, we could actually see Tubbie's aircraft silhouetted above the cloud; Alan couldn't avoid a comment to me that they seemed to be steering a slightly different course to us. To give Alan his due, he was certainly entitled to

question my ability against Doug Brown's. At the end of their conversation Alan couldn't resist saying, 'Tubbie' 'Yes Alan'. 'Course 098, Tubbie'. Back came the calm reply, 'I have a navigator too, Alan.' It was a good raid – we got an aiming point photo – but I got some stick from Doug Brown when we met in the interrogation room on return.

Whilst waiting around the squadron after Alan Craig left to go to 3 Group at the end of our second tour, I did four interesting ops with Wing Commander Brian Foster. A man of great courage, he had a very bad stammer on the ground which left him completely in the air when there was any emergency. The PFF used to occasionally do a raid completely on their own. We went to Koblenz on the night of November 21st, 1944, with no more than an effort of 25 aircraft, but with a significant difference – we had no markers. Having no main force to mark for, we had our bomb bays filled with HE's. Time over target was 0300 hours next morning. The Germans were used to seeing our raids take a set pattern. Illuminator flares dropped at H-minus-6; Red and Green TI's at H-minus-4; then the main force bombing, with TI's being replaced by the PFF, and directions coming from a Master Bomber. This night there were no markers, no illuminators; just a raid by blind bombing crews, who let them all go within 30 seconds of 0300. A few days previous we went to a place called Julich, and we were Master Bombers. Whilst directing the bombing after marking we were hit and on fire. Losing height, we turned for home. Two of the crew went to work on the fire and had it extinguished within 10 minutes. We weren't holding our height too well though. Throughout all this time Brian Foster never faltered in his speech. His orders were clear, concise, and calm. To my dismay, once the fire was out, he asked me for a course back to target. We went back, saw the raid completed, and returned home safe and sound.

The determination to be a highly skilled navigator with the Path Finder Force, who excelled in the art, replaced for me a civilian occupation totally. It was a completely absorbing task, in which one could lose oneself, and almost separate it from being anything to do with combat. Certainly the activity from take-off to landing was intense. The approaches to; time over; and departure period from target area, could be akin to a personal appearance before a firing squad, continuing indefinitely. I always found that an extra effort on the ground paid off handsomely in the air at the critical time. Following and understanding the build-up of the weather forecast during the day, so that the actual briefing before flight became an extension of what the Met Officer had already told you about the general situation. Generally speaking, it was a relentless slog to keep on top of the task. Keeping on track over the laid-down route out and back from a raid, usually being provided the protection from radar and flak which comes from being one of many aircraft which, although you could not see in the dark, their presence served as a chance that you would not be the one picked out. The skill of arriving at a target within 30 seconds of planned time, after several hours and hundreds of miles, was a necessary prerequisite of the whole Path Finder concept. There was no simple secret to this; just intensive effort to regularly find your position and revise and adjust as necessary. A successful navigation trip of $9\frac{1}{2}$ hours, to a place like Stettin, on time over the target, and back home again, could be very rewarding.

It was a unique form of existence, where the rather mundane responsibilities of payment of bills, home-building and upkeep were absent. Where daily routine simplified itself around one critical question – were you ON? If so, your attention was centred on preparing yourself effectively. Returning from a raid to sleep between sheets, with all mod cons seemed to me to make the whole existence somewhat bizarre. In the absence of any commitment on the battle order of the day, and once any training schedules had been discharged, there was the probability of a free evening,

usually with a prospect of good company and a really carefree atmosphere that is difficult, probably impossible to capture in a peacetime situation, particularly in civilian life. It was an existence that produced larger than life characters on a squadron, but – for the record – it was never one long laugh punctuated only by shallow thoughts. The recurring losses in the unit created a macabre situation, where one seldom saw comrades fall in battle, as in other arms of the forces; they just weren't around after everyone had returned. They had 'got the chop'. The attempts to treat such a very serious situation light-heartedly must have seemed faintly ridiculous to an outside observer.

Being a sentimentalist, I still pay occasional visits to Oakington. The field itself now grows grain. The approach past the bus stop and the church is still the same. When walking along the road between the church and what used to be the entrance, I am conscious of how often I trod the road before, in such different circumstances. The singing voices of a group of WAAFs returning from a pub on a night in June come ringing back down all those years – 'You can't expect eau-de-cologne from . . .' It was a Service song, more crude than I had been brought up to expect from female voices. Yet 30-odd years have given it respectability, and a light dignity . . .

Wing Commander S 'Tubby' Baker, DSO, DFC, who completed 100 operational sorties, and commanded 635 Squadron from July 1944 to March 1945./*Imperial War Museum*

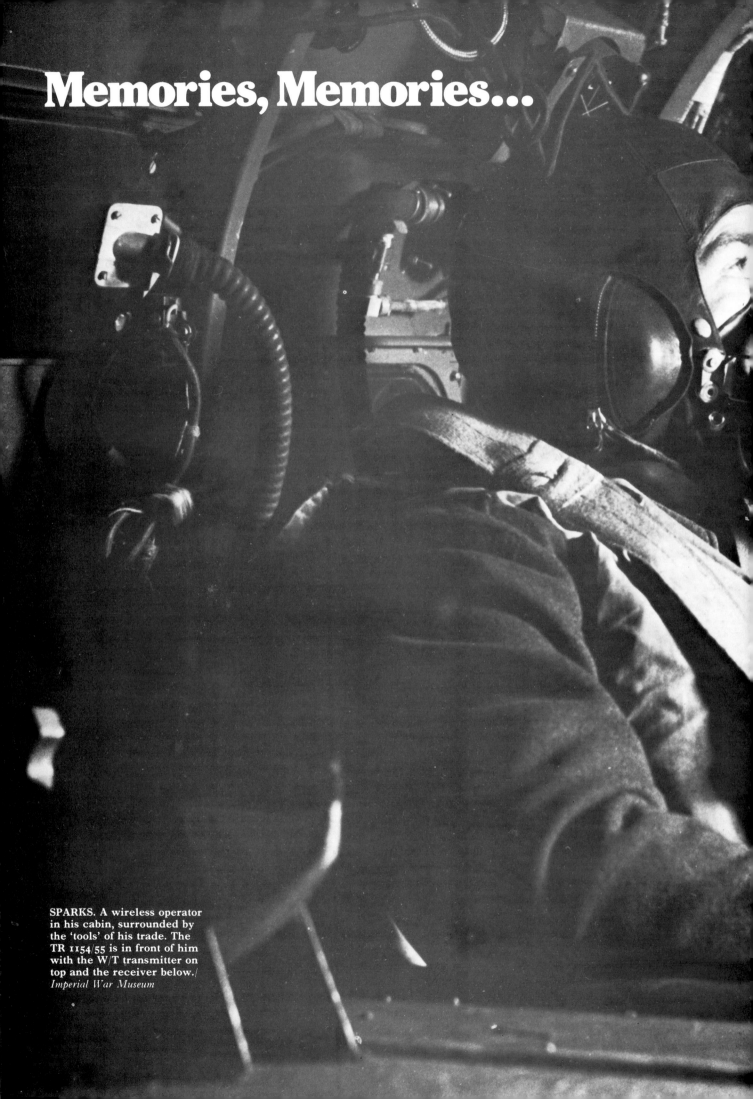

Memories, Memories...

SPARKS. A wireless operator in his cabin, surrounded by the 'tools' of his trade. The TR 1154/55 is in front of him with the W/T transmitter on top and the receiver below./
Imperial War Museum

To look back 30 years or more and try to recall details of one's youth and times is a severe test of memory, however well prompted by log books, records and photographs. To most air crews of the 1939-45 war, particularly the bomber crews, such delving into their past evokes memories of people primarily. Men who shared their own fears, tragedies, excitement; men with whom they had flown through the hell of flak and night fighters and seemingly survived by a miracle; men whose friendship was closer at times than blood relatives; and men – too often, mere boys – whose bright familiar faces were suddenly missing from their intimate community in the mess. Such nostalgia also very clearly recalls the 'good times' – parties, revels, off-duty adventures – testimony to the unconscious survival instinct born within every human. Even after deep thought and prodigious research, most ex-crew members only retain the bright facets of the overall picture – incidents and people who have claimed a permanent niche in the memory for a variety of reasons. Perhaps typical are the reminiscences of Bill Davies, an Englishman born and bred but now resident in Canada. A navigator II (or set operator), Davies completed a total of 43 operations with 156 Squadron, flying in Lancasters, during the final seven months of the war. His memories are fragmentary, perhaps, retrieving only the outstanding items and moments – all are marked indelibly on his mind.

I commenced operations in October 1944, but it is my opinion that we were not a good, well-disciplined crew up to and including an operation we did in T-Tommy (ND875) to Wilhelmshaven on October 15th, 1944. It was of four hours 40 minutes duration and take-off was at 1715 hours. I can remember few details except that we had a fire in the cockpit area with a fair bit of smoke. The bombs, no markers, were jettisoned in the countryside, and George Blick, the Nav 1, and I conspired to 'cook' the log. The following day in the navigation section we were called in by Squadron Leader Dixie Dean, the nav leader, and Squadron Leader Blackadder, the set operators' boss, I felt that we were before the late Mr Justice Humphries on a charge of mass murder! Dean and Blackadder were mature and sophisticated and in a few minutes we owned up – they were only too aware of what we had done. However, I think they treated us very well, and scared the pants off us by a threat that we might be thrown out of the Pathfinder Force. A crew meeting was held later and from that moment, I believe, we became a very effective crew indeed, with strong leadership from our skipper, Flying Officer F D Wallace (later, Flt Lt, DFC and tragically killed in India around 1947).

The following months comprised a fairly steady sequence of operations, but only particular ops come to mind in any detail. We had our fair share of 'incidents' but were, quite obviously, not alone in that respect. For example, on November 2nd, 1944 the squadron took off to bomb Dusseldorf and we were in T-Tommy. One of our Lancs was piloted by Sqn Ldr A W G Cochrane – 'Cocky' to his intimates – crashed on take-off with the undercarriage collapsed. Cocky was using a new flight engineer that night and, as was his habit, he talked to his aircraft, and rolling down the runway for the off, Cocky said, 'Up you bastard'. The flight engineer promptly lifted the undercart and the Lanc settled in beautifully – complete with a 4,000 lb 'Cookie' in the bomb bay! I believe a Pilot Officer Dee was his bomb aimer and the story gained credence that Cocky and crew fled the aircraft with phenomenal speed, but could not spot Dee until he approached them from the *opposite* direction, away from the aircraft. Dee explained that he was out and rolling like a ball when the Lanc was still doing 40mph! The cookie did not explode, but I remember several that did in similar circumstances – in the main force.

On January 16th, 1945, we took off in L-London (PB560) at 1818 hrs for Zeitz – duration 7 hrs 02 mins – as blind illuminators.

Right: BOMBER'S VIEW. Bomb aimer in a Lancaster, peering through the circular bombing panel fitted just beneath the nose gun turret.

Below: Typical 'fire' load for a Lancaster – a 4,000lb HC 'Cookie' blast bomb (centre rear position), nestling amongst a host of 500lb Cluster Incendiary 'bombs'.

On leaving the target after the new course to steer was given to the pilot, it was my habit to nip out from the navigation table for a few minutes as an extra pair of eyes in that dangerous situation. Leaving Zeitz I did just that. All aircraft on the raid without exception were supposed to fly at not higher than 18,000 feet. Nonetheless, that order was breached by the main force – it was frequently. A huge bomb, clearly visible – I am fairly certain it was a 4,000 lb cookie – just missed us in front of the starboard engines. Within about a minute three of us (pilot, engineer and myself) simultaneously saw a Halifax dead ahead, approaching us. The skipper frantically pushed the stick forward and the Halifax skimmed over the top of us at about 20 feet. What course that Hallie was steering was his own business but he could have been lost on the way and cut a corner when the crew saw our marking suddenly lighting the target.

Our only Politz operation, and particularly the homeward journey, is still vivid. It was February 8th, 1945, take-off 1924 hrs, duration 8 hrs 30 mins. We flew A-Apple (NG438) that night and acted as blind illuminators. We had just crossed the coast with a long stretch of cold North Sea ahead of us when the mid-upper gunner (Ff Off J McCrory) sang out that a Ju 88 was sitting out on the starboard beam with his cockpit

light on. McCrory immediately alerted us to the possibility of the Ju's friend who might sneak up behind, blacked out naturally. Sure enough a Ju 88 behind opened fire and shot out the engine providing power to the rear turret. A second engine was then knocked out but we escaped from the Ju's in cloud. Very shortly after a third engine just stopped and was duly feathered. I recall a conversation principally between the captain and our engineer, Sgt Eddie Ogden; the outcome of which was that nothing more could be done. We had been descending in a shallow glide from about 18,000 feet for some time and had levelled out, still on just one engine. At that point we were about 3-400 miles from base, having had a track home which crossed Sweden (quite 'illegal' of course). I remember a little flak near Malmo and, looking out, distinctly seeing the traffic lights! At all events it was a relatively high latitude track home resulting in the long North Sea route.

The skipper started talking about ditching, and subsequently told our wireless operator (Warrant Officer J T Barnes) that we should send an SOS (of our ditching position). Barnes replied that at 500 feet – our then height off the water – our radio range for an SOS was hopeless. More desultory conversation and the decision was made by the skipper to ditch. Blick and I used to wear ordinary shoes, not flying boots, and apart

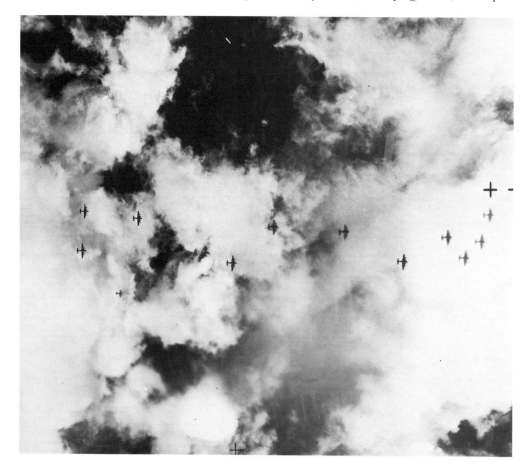

GOING OVER – part of the main stream of Lancasters, seen from 18,000 ft on July 19th, 1944.

from an ordinary battle dress, we were aware of the problem of exposure in the North Sea in January-February. Blick and I shook hands and wished each other good luck. Before we actually took up ditching positions, however, the engine that had stopped burst into action. Neither Wallace nor Eddie the engineer had a clue as to why. We returned on two engines. Most of the squadron were stacked up over base awaiting landing instructions when one aircraft asked for emergency landing permission on three engines. We then piped up and requested permission on two engines – it was immediately granted and we were down there very quickly. After de-briefing I went outside with McCrory for a cigarette – and promptly fainted!

Chemnitz was our target on February 14th, 1945. Take-off in T-Tommy (PB593) was at 2055 hrs, acting as blind sky markers with a duration of 7 hrs 45 mins. On the return journey we were attacked by an Me 262 jet. I nipped out from under the curtain and watched the proceedings from start to finish. We were attacked from the rear and I can still see clearly the lazy, long bluish cannon tracer snaking towards us and just missing the port tailplane. I vividly recall the discipline of the crew. Everyone kept silent except Michael McCrory (the only Canadian in our crew, the rest being English). McCrory gave the captain the corkscrew instructions. Both the mid-upper and the rear gunner – a kindly, lovable, quiet man who we thought was really old – Sgt James Hayton, then about 35 or 36 years old, were banging away with their six .303 Brownings. A tremendous racket and the usual stink of cordite. The gunners got a superb hit exactly in the starboard wingroot of the jet and the entire starboard wing fell off. The jet then just plunged in flames and I lost sight of it. None of us saw a parachute but it was a fairly dark night and there was every possibility, unless the pilot was hit, that he was able to eject. Both George Blick and I made adequate entries of the time, heights, position etc and our crew were shortly after informed that the incident was fully confirmed by one or more aircraft from 35 Squadron. Only then did we paint the swastika on our Lanc T-Tommy and I wrote 'Confirmed' in the log book.

Speaking more generally, there was a widespread feeling on 156 Squadron of immense pride in being in the Pathfinder Group, and we were all sure it extended to all squadrons in 8 Group. One could not imagine morale to be higher, and any thought of going back to the main force was looked on as akin to the end of the world. When Wing Commander T L Bingham-Hall, DSO, DFC, was taken off ops and posted to a desk job at Air Ministry it must have been a terrible jolt for him. All aircrew had 'prayers', the name for a

LIGHTING UP TIME. A Lancaster of 156 Squadron releasing its TI's over Hanau on 18/19th March, 1945. The brilliance of the multi-coloured pyrotechnics silhouettes another Lancaster below as the 'Christmas Trees' cascade down.

squadron aircrew meeting, one morning and he was presented with a silver cigarette case. Tears were rolling down his cheeks during his little speech of thanks and he could hardly speak. It was all very moving. He was succeeded by Wg Cdr D B Falconer, DFC, AFC, who was lost on December 30th, 1944 over Cologne; and eventually command of 156 went to Wg Cdr Alan J L Craig, DSO, DFC, a very fine officer indeed and well respected and liked.

One unusual incident comes to mind; it occurred at briefing one night. We had all crowded into the huge briefing room, the curtain concealing the map of Europe was drawn back, and the target revealed. It was a very deep penetration job, though I cannot recall the specific target. During the briefing it was said that none other than Don Bennett himself had ordered that we do a circuit of, I believe, Brunswick, *on the way* to the target. What the purpose was escapes me but it may have been for 'training purposes'. At all events everyone started to bitch and complain, and quite openly too – which was unusual, not to say without precedent. Several section leaders left the stage and a few minutes later returned to cancel that little circuit nonsense. It was said they had telephoned Bennett. The general impression I had was that Bennett was God himself. They said he had written a book on navigation in three

parts – one part for beginners, one for advanced students, and one for AVM Bennett because he was the only one who could understand it. It was also said of Bennett that he believed that anyone shot down could and should get back to base within a month – after all he had done it! We did not see him too often but everyone loved him and had a grave respect for his ability.

Life had its lighter moments, of course. Always, but always we were constantly urinating on the way *to* a target – never on the way home! Consequently, as all crews did, we carried a large can, maybe of two-gallon size, and this was passed around up front constantly. Now it was the flight engineer's job in our aircraft to shoot out the 'Window' (anti-radar foil strips) from an aperture in the nose. The 'Window' consisted of packages and one can readily appreciate that the package having some bulk and weight could be dropped without problems. So, when one night the can of urine was filled almost to the brim and needed emptying, Eddie Ogden was designated to do this. He proceeded to simply pour it all in one quick movement down the aperture. Unfortunately it all came back and soaked him completely, head, shoulders, arms, body – the works. I never heard such language in my life before – and at least Eddie quickly discovered who his true friends were!

Left: **NAVIGATOR'S UNION PARTY – a gathering of navigators of 156 Squadron hold a 'union meeting', with PFF boss – and chief navigator, Don Bennett, as chief guest. Second photo shows, left to right, 156 Squadron's commander; Don Bennett; and the Upwood station commander – suitably attired . . ./***R V Dickeson***, DFC

Above: One for the family album – a 156 crew pose for a studio photographer. L-R: Flt Lt R V Dickeson, DFC (Navigator); Sqn Ldr P P Hague, DFC & Bar (Skipper); Flt Lt H 'Jack' Ramsay, DFC (Radar Operator); and Fg Off J O'Brien (Rear Air Gunner)./***R V Dickeson***, DFC**

Night of the Jet Stream

THEY ALSO SERVE . . . just
a few of the many
thousands of anonymous and
seldom publicised erks –
ground crews – whose
labours produced the
serviceable aircraft without
fail. A Lancaster
maintenance crew pose with
their charge after its return
from a sortie to Berlin./
Imperial War Museum

On the night of March 24/25th, 1944, Bomber Command mounted the final operation of the so-termed 'Battle of Berlin', despatching over 700 bombers to the 'Big City'. Of these 72 aircraft (9.1 per cent of the total force) were lost; about 50 of these to the flak defences not only of Berlin but of several other towns and cities many miles from the planned bomber route. The cause was an unknown (till then) phenomena – jet streams in the upper atmosphere. In general the navigators that night became bemused by seemingly impossible wind velocities indicated by their calculations, and this factor, combined with a refusal by headquarters in England to believe the true figures radioed to them by the leading PFF aircraft, plus a certain amount of tardiness in overall communications between HQ and the main bomber formations, led to a disastrous loss rate. One of the PFF crews who 'discovered' this phenomena was that of Lancaster ME620, C-Charlie of 35 Squadron. Skippered by Pilot Officer L S White (later, Flt Lt, DFC), its crew comprised Plt Off H C Wright (later Sqn Ldr, DFC as navigator – 'Nav One'; F.Sgt R Everest (later Fg Off, DFM), set operator – 'Nav Two'; F.Sgt R Bull (Fg Off, DFC), wireless operator; Sgt W Smith (WO, DFM & BAR), Flight engineer; F.Sgt A Williams (WO, DFC), Rear gunner; and Sgt J Levett (WO, DFM), mid-upper gunner.

'It was the evening of March 24th, 1944,

BIG BANG. A 4,000lb HC 'Cookie' awaiting loading into Lancaster L7540, OL-U, of 83 Squadron at Wyton, 1942. This view shows the 'tail' section.

and at Graveley airfield the briefing was almost over. The white tape marking the bombers' route that night extended right across the massive operations map, from base to Berlin and back again to base, feinting first in the direction of a German city on the way out and then to another, but always avoiding the large red blobs en route which indicated areas of intense hostility. The biggest blob was Berlin itself. The crews of 35 Squadron were listening to the end of the met officer's briefing. 'As you see, the winds are going to be a bit tricky and that is why we have given you wind velocities in four stages on the way out, and five stages on the way back. Your timed bombing runs have been worked out using a wind velocity of 360/52 knots, which is what it's expected to be in the target area. As the navigation leader has told you, the two primary markers, C-Charlie and G-George, will be zephyring, and if there are any appreciable differences from the forecast winds the gen will be broadcast in flight.'

Zephyring was a device often used on long flights to assist the bombers to achieve maximum concentration. There was safety in numbers if the bombers kept as close as possible in both time and space, and the object was to get the maximum number of bombers over the target in the shortest possible period of time. If navigators used incorrect wind velocities in their calculations they became separated from the main bomber stream; prey to predicted flak and fighters, and if they got to the target at all they probably arrived late. Zephyring enabled the whole bomber force to call on the experience of selected Pathfinder crews who were detailed to report to HQ by radio on the wind velocities which they had found. If the winds reported by the Pathfinders differed appreciably from the forecast winds, they were re-broadcast to the crews in the air.

Briefing and flight preparations over, the crews dispersed to their aircraft to carry out pre-flight drills and checks. One by one the snarl of engines from the farthest corners of the airfield proclaimed that 35 Squadron's Lancasters were ready to 'do battle'. On other airfields all over England that evening 450 other bomber crews were going through the same motions.

Lancaster C-Charlie was the first to take off, and as it lumbered into the night sky its navigator noted the fact in his log and gave the pilot his first course. The first leg to Cromer was short and, crossing the coast, the Lanc turned gently to port and continued climbing into the dark over the North Sea. Whilst most of the crew adjusted to the relative inactivity of a two-hour sea crossing, the navigators in their dimly lit compartment had plenty to do. 'Nav Two to Nav One.

The coast is just disappearing from the screen. Here's a last fix from Cromer. Ready? 060 degrees, 21 miles.' 'Nav One to Nav Two, the forecast winds seem to be OK so far but it's early yet. Try the GEE box for a little while before it gets jammed. Let me have your last reliable fix before you lose the signals and we'll see where that puts us.' After a short while Nav Two responded, 'This is the last GEE fix you'll get. It's disappearing into the mush. Here it is, 53.27 North 02.08 East.' Nav One worked out the wind and gave the pilot a slight alteration of course. Half an hour passed in silence except for small talk between crew members, then 'Nav One to Captain. We're now at position A by dead reckoning. Alter course to 063 degrees. ETA enemy coast 21.08.5.' 'Let me know when we are 15 miles from the coast' was the reply. The skipper always made this request because he liked to start weaving gently from side to side before reaching the coast. It made the job of enemy radar that much harder and gave solace of a sort to the crew. Nav One had already allowed for it in his flight plan by deducting four knots from the air speed.

The only other navigational item which had to be recorded during the next hour was a message from the skipper, '19,000 feet and levelling out.' C-Charlie with its heavy load had reached its operational height. The 'inactivity' was about to end. 'Nav Two to Nav One. Enemy coast coming up on radar but I don't recognise it yet. It looks like Sylt about 20 miles away on the port side. It IS Sylt, quite definitely.' . . . 'Can't be. Sylt should be well over to starboard.' . . . 'Look for yourself. We'll be passing directly over Nordstrand in about four minutes.' . . . 'Nav One to Captain. There's something screwy here somewhere; we're 50 miles south of track. What course are you flying?' . . . '063 degrees, the course you told me to fly' . . . 'OK Alter course now to 020 degrees while I work something out.' During this interchange Nav Two had plotted a fix from Nordstrom and with this information Nav One worked out the wind velocity. Speaking to nobody in particular he flicked over his microphone switch and, in tones of utter disbelief. announced, 'Impossible! I've got a wind of 012/115 knots!' and then after a pause, 'Something must be on the blink. Engineer please go down the back and check the gyro.' 'There's flak on both sides of us' – this from the rear gunner. 'Flak ships and coastal guns. At least we are somewhere in the middle of the stream' – a comforting thought from the skipper. The flight engineer puffed his way back from the depths of the fuselage and, plugging in his oxygen and intercomm, said, 'Engineer here. The gyro is OK'. 'Then it just has to be 012/115 knots. Wireless operator

please zephyr 012/115 knots to start with. Nav One to Captain, keep on 020 for the time being. We're flying into the wind and making little headway. It'll take us too long to rejoin our original track but this course will cut off a large corner and bring us to our required track for the next leg into the Baltic. We should then be OK again for time but I'll check.'

Apart from pinpoint accuracy as markers, Pathfinders had to be immaculate timekeepers, with a tolerance of six minutes either side of their allotted bombing time. To achieve this precision Pathfinders set course from their bases with three minutes in hand for every hour of flying time to the target. In this way they had time in hand for unforeseen snags such as this. Usually they did not require the extra time and had to get rid of it by flying short dog legs, but on this occasion C-Charlie needed all the time and more. After what to the crew seemed an eternity, C-Charlie reached the new track without further incident and altered course to 094 to take them to the next turning point at Gedser on the island of Falster in the Baltic Sea.

'Wireless Operator to Nav One. The wind velocity being broadcast is 020/70 knots' . . . 'What the hell are they playing at? Who's wrong, us or them? We're on track, we're on time, and we're using a wind of 012/120. We can't have this wind all to ourselves. I wonder what t'other zephyr aircraft has sent? Let's check it again'. The Lancaster by now was close to the island of Aero and Nav Two was busy plotting fixes on its southern tip. 'Take a new fix now. 172 degrees Aero 12 miles.' Nav One noted the fix, the time and the

ON THE BUTTON.
Lancaster bomb aimer, sighting through the revised, enlarged aiming panel introduced in Lancs with the B.III version; and holding the 'tit' (bomb release button)./*Ministry of Defence (Air)*

reading on the Air Position Indicator and worked out his wind. '004/135 knots. If it gets any stronger we may find ourselves going backwards. Wireless operator, please zephyr 004/135 knots.' . . . 'There seems to be quite a chop going on south of us' – again it was the laconic Willie in the rear turret . . . 'That's where everybody is. We're probably up here all by ourselves' – this was 'Confucius', the mid-upper gunner. . . . 'Not on your life. There's air to air over here on the port. Somebody's on fire.' . . . 'Shut up', admonished the skipper, 'Keep a sharp watch. We're in Yellow Nose country and these boys are vicious.' . . . 'Wireless Op to Nav One, they're now broadcasting 020/80 knots' . . . 'Let them get stuffed then. They just don't believe me. Anyway, we're using 135 knots and getting there. I'm not sending any more winds if they don't want them.'

The course brought C-Charlie directly over Gedser where it turned on to a new course of 117 degrees to take it to a point 40 miles north-east of Berlin. The route had been planned deliberately to pass over the large lakes at Demmin, Neubrandenberg and Prenzlau, situated at about 25 minute intervals, which provided excellent radar signals for the navigators to check their final winds and speeds. Things were hotting up around them. Opposition was mounting. They made it to the last turning point without incident except they had to get rid of three minutes 20 seconds of surplus time due to the strength of the wind on their port quarter, and their anticipated ground speed on the final leg.

'Nav One to Captain. Alter course to target. 222 degrees. The wind is right up our tail and our ground speed is 342 knots. We'll be there smack on time at 22.25' . . . 'Nav Two to Captain. We can't drop the TI's, they'd be miles off before they ignited and would drift downwind for miles whilst they were burning. I'm selecting bombs only' . . . 'Agreed. We're coming up quite quickly. Somebody's got there already. The party has started'.

The metropolitan area of Berlin, the large red blobs on the Ops Room map back at base, was about 20 miles across and massively defended. The sky above the city was being combed by searchlights and rent by a myriad flak bursts which, at this distance and at first sight, appeared as an impenetrable curtain right in the path of the bombers. The flight path across the city took about five minutes at normal bombing speeds, but tonight with that fantastic wind behind it C-Charlie would take only three minutes. The crew were thankful for small mercies!

'We're coming up to aiming point' (Nav Two was bombing by radar on a timed run from a radar fix). Bomb doors open. Hold this course'. Crisis point had been reached. The flak bursts were very close. Nav Two was counting, 'Ten seconds . . . five seconds, four, three, two, one, bombs gone' . . . 'Alter course 230 degrees magnetic. Short run to next turning point.' Nav One was loath to interfere with the business of leaving the scene as quickly as possible. Nose down, C-Charlie roared out of the target area and after a few minutes turned onto a course of 294 degrees, the first of the homeward legs. The target area was still near enough for the crew to see the fires, the smoke, the brickdust and the brilliant explosions. They could also see that a quantity of flares and a few TI's were by now adding

Two views of Berlin. (Right) a TI bursting and seen from 27,000 ft by Flt Lt Baldwin in Mosquito 'F' of 139 Squadron on July 7/8th, 1944. (Far right) twin markers' illumination, and the weird effects of icy air produced this view of Berlin on July 7/8th, 1944, as seen from Mosquito 'J' of 139 Squadron, flown by Fg Off Richard at 27,000 ft.

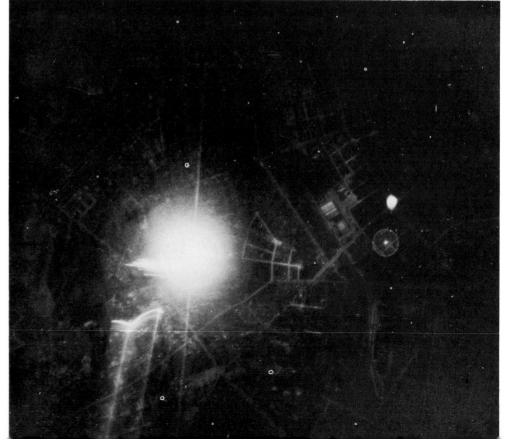

to the lurid confusion. The skipper was first to comment, 'It's certainly not a 400-bomber effort but at least somebody got there in spite of the duff winds. They must have used their own. I'm afraid the TI's will attract a good bit of bombing.'

Homeward journeys were always more relaxed. The skipper could put up the revs a bit and there was no bother about time-keeping. C-Charlie was purring along beautifully. Not that there was anything to get complacent about. There was still a fighter-infested continent to cross, not to speak of a nasty sea crossing and the continuing problem of that wind. After circumnavigating Magdeburg, Hanover and Osnabruck, the flight plan was routed over Holland and out to sea. The navigators watched the radar screen in silence as the bomber crossed the Zuider Zee and the last strand of enemy territory passed beneath them. That was the supreme moment, the exhilarating thrill of survival. The flight engineer again disappeared into the bowels of the aircraft but this time returned with flasks of coffee. It was a ritual. Losing height rapidly C-Charlie headed for Cromer and Nav One was prudent enough to consult the lower level winds which he had found on the early stages of the flight out.

C-Charlie arrived over base at 01.06 and was the first of the brood to return. At the briefing, sipping a tot of rum, Nav One spoke of the fantastic winds and of his chagrin when they had not been acted upon. The skipper reckoned that the chop rate for the night would be high. The CO reached across for Nav One's log, glanced through it ruefully and handed it back without a word. Two of his crews had not yet returned. The Navigation officer explained that nobody at HQ was prepared to believe the winds. The other zephyring aircraft did not send any at all – it was one of the aircraft that had not yet returned.

Just after the war ended Nav One, by then a civilian, was invited to the Royal Geographical Society HQ in London to hear an eminent lecturer give a talk on jet streams. At this time the practical uses of such phenomena were just beginning to be realised in aviation circles, and there was a sprinkling of RAF and civil aviation top brass in the audience. Although jet streams at such comparatively low altitudes are unusual, it was the misfortune of the aircraft of Bomber Command that night, unwittingly, to fly into the lower levels of such streams. The lecturer was quite definite about it. He started his lecture by saying that the first knowledge that the world ever had of the existence of jet streams was when the bombers returned from Berlin in the early hours of March 25th, 1944. Illustrating his words with a slide showing the spread of the bomber stream, all over Europe, he said, 'The winds encountered by the bombers were so abnormally strong that navigators doubted their own instruments and calculations. The result was that they used the wrong winds and the bomber force was scattered over a wide area of the continent. A large number never returned.' On that fateful night the crew of Lancaster C-Charlie were not aware of it, nor may not have given it much thought since, but they could justifiably claim to be the first human beings to become aware of the existence of jet streams – at least, Nav One likes to think so . . .

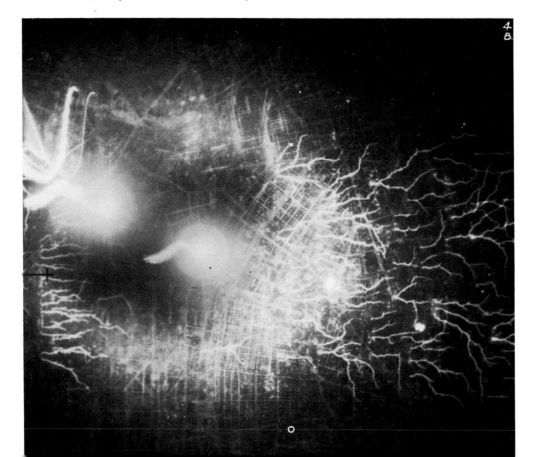

Nav's View
GEOFF WHITTEN

Halifax I, W7676, P-Peter of
35 Squadron, displaying one
of the early jet-black
undersurfaces finishes.
| Aeroplane

After training as a navigator in Canada, I began operations with 78 Squadron in 4 Group, flying Halifaxes from Linton-on-Ouse, near York, in November 1942, about five weeks after my 22nd birthday. After 20 sorties I was 'persuaded' to join a crew who had volunteered to transfer to Pathfinder Force but were minus a navigator – he having declined to go with them. The skipper was Jimmy Davidson, and bomb aimer S R (Tim) Green; all three of us being lowly Pilot Officers. When, on arrival at 35 Squadron based at Graveley on March 14th, 1943, we realised we were to be introduced to the mysteries of H2S, we had no difficulty in deciding that I would do the plotting, and Tim would become the set operator. All three of us quickly developed a good and happy understanding as the nucleus of what I think I can describe as a fairly typical Pathfinder crew of that particular era – professional without being pompous about it; conscientious without unnecessary heroics; and, perhaps above all, sufficiently resilient and mutually supporting to be able to maintain (at least, outwardly) cheerfulness and morale at a high level despite all the strains.

Like most other Pathfinder crews we pretended to be 'press-on' types, but I would not *now* pretend that we were star performers at the job we'd taken on, and certainly not that we were ever disposed to reckless bravery. For instance, I clearly recall a raid on Cologne in June 1943 when we took such a pounding from the flak while 'coned' on the approach to the target, that none of us dissented from the only decision we ever made to dump the bomb load and get the hell out of it. On the other hand (if only to illustrate the quirks of human nature . . .), on a less hazardous trip to Le Creusot three days later, we lost an engine before we reached enemy territory and quite cheerfully flew the rest of the way there and back on three. And I suppose that the fact that we survived 20 PFF operations as an intact crew (all ending as officers with gongs) showed that we must have had *some* skill as well as luck. Most of us had subsequent trips with other crews, and Jimmy and Tim added bars to their DFCs. On the subject of luck, I will admit immediately that in those 20 ops we did not see an enemy fighter within gun range. Flak, however, was something we could never escape. Flying straight and level up to and beyond the target for marking, and then flash photography, was never a picnic in a Halifax with its lower ceiling and slower speed than a Lancaster. And when doing primary marking at the head of the stream, before the defences were swamped, left one feeling very naked indeed.

On the question of heading the stream, I recall one raid which was a nerve-wracking experience for another reason. Having passed our apprenticeship as Pathfinders, after two

months of H2S training and a few operations in a minor role, we found ourselves promoted to primary markers for an attack on Pilsen on May 13, 1943. This entailed a very long trip across the heart of Germany and into Czechoslovakia, with little on the way to help much with navigation. The main force, whose navigational problems were even worse, were to be helped by Pathfinder aircraft dropping markers at the last turning point before the target. We were flying in Halifax II, JB786 for this op and as the appointed time – and the supposed place – for this marking approached we grew more and more anxious, because for all we could see in the Stygian blackness surrounding us there wasn't another aircraft, enemy or friendly, within 50 miles of us. When Tim and I decided we'd reached the turning point it was already past the scheduled time, yet we seemed to be all alone.

A gentle orbit to allow a few minutes for someone older and bolder to put down a marker produced nothing within sight, so at last we dropped ours and set course for the target, hoping desperately that we had not just led several hundred assorted heavies astray. Soon our tail gunner reported other markers going down, some near ours and others at various points of the compass and distances from it. We were in almost an identical dilemma when we reached what we identified, with no great certainty, .as the

target. However, by this time some of the other marking aircraft had caught up with us and the marking, though scattered geographically, was at least not so solitary.

In the event we did not even have the satisfaction of emerging from our maiden marking operation with any credit; the raid turned out to have been a failure, with most of the bombs having fallen on a neighbouring town rather than on Pilsen itself. Presumably there was no photographic evidence to point the finger, but we had contributed to the fiasco. Such failures, I may say, were taken very seriously by Pathfinder crews themselves, though not more seriously than by our boss, Don Bennett – I remember with some chagrin his reaction to the misfiring of a raid on Hanover in September that year (by which time our original crew had split up and I was 'filling in' with other crews).

The day after the raid on Pilsen all pilots, navigators and set operators of the marking crews were summoned to Group HQ at Wyton, where Don Bennett conducted a most clinically-cold postmortem. He had already had all the navigation logs sent to him and had worked through them all to discover where each of us had gone wrong. It was not very pleasant to have our errors publicly exposed by someone whose knowledge of air navigation brooked no contradiction.

In case it should appear that I'm hinting at

MASTER OF CEREMONIES. Group Captain John Searby (centre) 83 Squadron, who was aerial 'director' of the massive raid on Peenemunde ('Operation Hydra') on August 17/18th, 1943; on which 597 heavy bombers were despatched, though 40 failed to return. It was the occasion too for the first operational use of 'Red Spot Fire' markers – a 250lb crimson flare TI. With Searby here are (left) Sqn Ldr R J Manton, later lost over Leipzig on October 20th, 1943, and Sqn Ldr Shaw; whilst in background is Lancaster B.III, JB114, 'Q2' of 83 Squadron.

too many failures by our 'typical PFF crew', I should mention one incident quite definitely against ourselves. On only our third evening at Graveley we were sent up with a number of other experienced crews to fly round and round a nearby bombing range while someone else set off a wide variety of new types of target markers. On our return we were to give a considered evaluation of their effectiveness. Not unnaturally, our 'evaluation' began in the air, with all crews expressing their opinions as each marker appeared. As some of the offerings were ludicrously inadequate the views expressed over our intercomms were often couched in language that would have to be considerably cleaned up before translation into the formal report at de-briefing. Unfortunately, the 'uncensored' version of the reactions of our very new PFF crew was already public property long before we got back to base – the whole of our conversation over the range had been broadcast live on our R/T! There were, we were told, blushing WAAFs in control towers over a wide area of East Anglia, as well as many apoplectic duty controllers who had tried in vain to get us off the air. The mitigating circumstances that, after all the uproar, allowed us to get away with this gaffe for nothing more than a reprimand, were that 35 Squadron aircraft were strange to us – one 80-minute flight was all that we'd had up to then – and the stranger

fact that, although otherwise identical in the cockpit to those we had flown on 78 Squadron, 35's Halifaxes had the R/T transmit/receive switch on the steering column rigged in the opposite direction. Jimmy, our skipper, had of course realised this but, unfortunately, had overlooked it at the vital moment.

One operation which stands out particularly was the now famous raid on Peenemunde V-weapon research station on August 17th, 1943. We were very powerfully briefed on the vital importance that the operation should succeed, with an implicit threat that anything but a complete knockout would only mean repeated and evermore dangerous attempts to wipe out a target of which we were not told the exact nature. The raid was to be carried out in full moon and at a relatively low level, with no great prospect of cloud cover on a route across Denmark and up the Baltic. As it turned out, the whole operation took place in what seemed like a vast floodlit arena. That night we flew in Halifax HR879. Navigators were usually kept so unremittingly busy that they had little chance to see what was going on around them. As far as I was concerned this was the chief attraction of being a navigator; being curtained off in my dimly-lit cubbyhole with my charts, dividers, pencils and log, was not only less boring than spending interminable hours peering into blackness, but was also a good deal less frightening than having

The combination of target indicators' illumination, searchlights, flak bursts, and the pink glare of a burning target, all combined to disperse the cloak of darkness in which the bombers preferred to operate; thereby making them clearly defined targets for flak and roving Luftwaffe night fighters. An example is this Halifax, silhouetted sharply, over Leipzig on the night of December 3rd/4th, 1943. / *Imperial War Museum*

to watch the action getting hotter and closer. On this raid, however, the navigation was undemanding, what with the visibility and the profusion of coasts and islands so easily identifiable on the 'box', that I was able to spend much more time than usual looking through the cockpit perspex or astro-dome.

What I saw was as terrifying as it was fascinating. In all the time we flogged up the Baltic and back there hardly seemed to be a minute in which somewhere around us there was not an aircraft in trouble, or burning, or exploding. Being back-up markers this time, we were about a third of the way from the front of the stream and therefore felt much more in the thick of it than usual. Over the target itself the raid seemed to be going well, though the Master of Ceremonies (John Searby of 83 Squadron) seemed to be far from satisfied with the efforts of the backers-up to keep the aiming point moving forward instead of back. Soon after our markers went down we heard him shouting, 'Ignore that last green' – we didn't *think* it was ours, but couldn't be certain it wasn't.

In 1943 accurate and reliable navigation over Europe at night was still not to be taken for granted. The relatively new H2S equipment gave a pack of trouble, both technically and operationally. Even when a set was working well, it took a lot of skill to interpret the images on the screen and a fiendish amount of concentration to keep moving from one identified feature to the next. Away from coastlines the task was almost impossible without very close co-operation and co-ordination between plotter and operator; and happy the crew (as ours was) in which these two had a good understanding. The unofficial navigators' 'union' was very strong in PFF, presumably because of the obvious critical importance of navigation to the Group's effectiveness and also because there were virtually two navigators in each crew, compared with one nav and one bomb aimer in main force aircraft.

It was a fairly general rule, at least on 35 Squadron, that the navigation team did not defer *too* much to the captain – although I suppose there had to be some deference when the latter was clearly more experienced than, and/or senior to the rest of the crew. Tim Green and I certainly acted on what is now called the need-to-know principle, believing that too much navigation information fed to the rest of the crew only led to misunderstanding and, sometimes, unnecessary alarm and despondency. Thus we were never lost – only temporarily uncertain of our position. And we *never* said, for an instance, 'We're 10 miles north of track. Correction course now being calculated.' From long experience, and not only with our own captain, we knew that few pilots given such information could resist

Daylight attacks towards the end of the war proved possible because of the air superiority held by the Allied air forces. Precision bombing in tactical support of the Allied armies advancing through Europe became a priority; as can be seen here – an attack on marshalling rail yards at Douai on August 11th, 1944 by 35 Squadron, from just over 14,000 ft.

Above: ERKS. The Instrument 'Bashers' of 35 & 692 Squadrons at Graveley, July 1945. Back row, l-r: Cpl Roneoff; Wilson; Foreman; Cpl Skinner; Bull; Crossland; Cpl Vallis; Cpl Eade; Flt Sgt L Woodhead, NCO i/c; Ireland; Stiff; Cavanagh; Warr; Cpl Fisher; Pyke; Cpl Breakner. Front row: Freeman; Unknown; Laurie; Cpl Cox; New; Murdoch; ACW Sproggen; Calder; Davies; Cpl Prosty (?); Walton. In background, a 35 Squadron Lancaster. / L Woodhead

Right: VETERANS. A 35 Squadron PFF crew. Standing, L-R, are Bob Lamb; Gordon Carter, DFC; Squadron Leader Julian Sale, DSO, DFC; Flt Lt Bodnar, DFC; Flt Sgt Cross, DFM; and Fg Off Rogers, DFC. Kneeling in front, the ground crew of their Halifax. Carter had the near-unique experience of being twice shot down in enemy territory, and evading capture on both occasions./G Carter, DFC

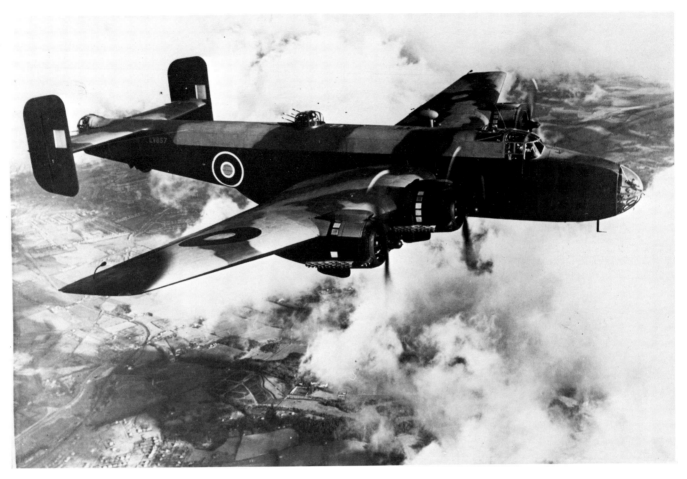

the temptation to begin surreptitiously edging to the south, with the result that by the time he'd been given the correction course we would be almost back on track and would soon find ourselves drifting south of it. As far as we were concerned the new course was given first and the reason for it only reluctantly followed if asked for.

My own conversion to the minimum-gen policy dated from an incident on one homeward-bound journey when the crew were especially persistent with the familiar query. 'How much longer to the enemy coast, navigator?'. There was audible relief all round when at length I was able to announce that we were just crossing the Dutch coast, though because of cloud there was nothing to be seen below. A few minutes later, with everyone winding down nicely, a solitary burst of flak, very near us, shattered the calm and, although that was all there was to it, the reaction to the shock was an outpouring of wrath and invective on the puzzled head of the poor old navigator. Backtracking later, I discovered that at the time I believed we had reached the North Sea we were actually approaching – all on our own – the defences of Rotterdam. Though this was a comparatively small error after several hours above 10/10ths cloud, my real mistake, I decided, was not keeping my beliefs to myself.

Two other incidents which occurred on 35 Squadron, though not involving me directly, are prominent in my memory. The first concerned a couple of especially gallant Canadian officers, Julian Sale and Gordon Carter, pilot and navigator respectively. Julian was rumoured to be a wealthy business man – it was even said that in his billet he had a whole row of immaculate uniforms. Gordon had already been shot down once but had evaded capture and got back to England. (I think I'm right in saying that later he did it again and ended up marrying the French girl who had helped him; after the war he played a leading part in UNICEF). Julian having also been shot down, evaded, and returned once, he and Gordon had a common bond of understanding. On December 20th, 1943, I and my crew mates were already safely down from a raid when Sale's Halifax arrived on the circuit with a blazing fire in its bomb bay – a TI had been triggered off, apparently. Sale ordered his crew to bale out and was about to follow suit when his mid-upper gunner, Bob Lamb, appeared beside him holding a charred parachute. Sale dropped back into his seat, stuck his head out of the port window (his cockpit was filled with smoke) and calmly took the Hallie round for a normal circuit landing. Roaring off the runway, the Halifax crashed neatly in a ball of fire; Sale and his

Halifax B.III, LV857 – a version fitted with Bristol Hercules XVI radial engines, in place of the earlier Merlin in-lines. Other modifications included the squared-off rudders; slightly increased wing span; retractable tail wheel; and an all round better operating performance. This version first entered service at the end of 1943./*Handley Page Ltd*

gunner got away safely, and the aircraft exploded. Julian got a bar to his DSO for this effort, but was I believe lost soon after. (*Squadron Leader J Sale, DSO, DFC was lost on February 20th, 1944, en route to Leipzig, being shot down by a Wunstorf-based Ju 88 nightfighter. Gordon Carter baled out successfully and again evaded capture . . . Author*)

The other incident concerned one of 35's more extrovert crews at this time, skippered by a pilot called Petrie-Andrews, whose navigator was Jack Armitage. They ran into trouble over an Italian target (Turin, I think) and, realising they could not get back over the Alps, set off for North Africa. Eventually they ditched in the Mediterranean somewhere near Corsica but were picked up by an Allied vessel and completed the crossing by sea. In due course they were found a Lancaster left at one of the North Africa bases after a shuttle raid and were despatched back to England in it. Justifiably expecting a rapturous welcome when they landed at Graveley, they thought to set the right tone for the coming

celebrations by giving their home airfield a comprehensive beat-up at virtually nought feet. They could not have known, of course, that at the very time they started the roofs rattling a very senior brasshat from Air Ministry was reaching the climax of a stern lecture to the squadron's flying personnel assembled in the crew room. The subject of his lecture was the criminal lunacy of unauthorised low flying and the severe measures now being put into force to stop it. Thus, Petrie-Andrews and his merry men stepped out of their borrowed Lanc – incidentally crammed to the main spar with a cargo of Arab carpets, flagons of wine, fruit galore and the like – to be greeted not with rapture but an embarrassed station commander armed with orders to place them all under immediate arrest. Although they spent the next few days confined to their quarters – surrounded, albeit by their exotic cargo – the threatened court martial never took place. Presumably someone in high places – wisely – thought better of it.

Left: Halifax I (Merlin engined) bombers fresh from the factory, waiting on Warton airfield near Preston, Lancashire, for delivery to the RAF. The nearest machine, JB899, went to 405 Squadron RCAF and served with the PFF. /English Electric Company

Below: Halifax Mk II, R9534, which was converted to become the prototype Mk III. Of particular interest here is the rear gun turret – the Automatic Gun Laying Turret (AGLT), with twin .50 machine guns, known to Bomber Command as 'Village Inn'. It automatically sighted and fired at an enemy aircraft, but very few had reached the operational squadrons before the war's end in Europe. /Crown Copyright

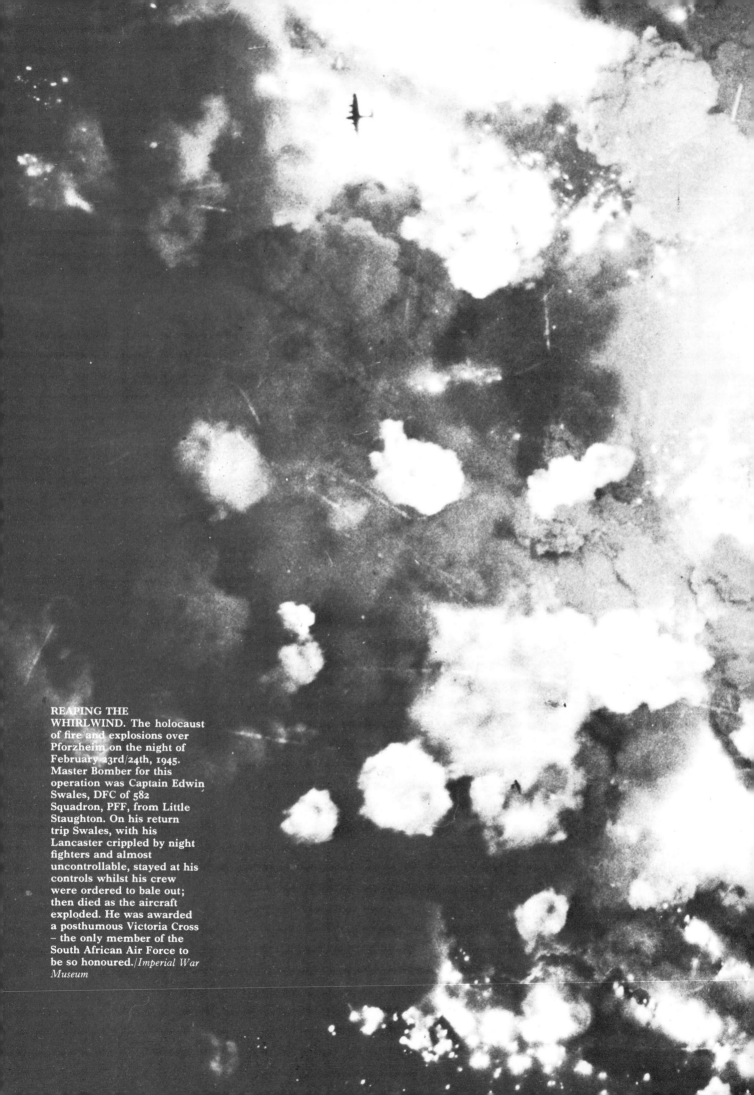

REAPING THE WHIRLWIND. The holocaust of fire and explosions over Pforzheim on the night of February 23rd/24th, 1945. Master Bomber for this operation was Captain Edwin Swales, DFC of 582 Squadron, PFF, from Little Staughton. On his return trip Swales, with his Lancaster crippled by night fighters and almost uncontrollable, stayed at his controls whilst his crew were ordered to bale out; then died as the aircraft exploded. He was awarded a posthumous Victoria Cross – the only member of the South African Air Force to be so honoured./*Imperial War Museum*

Night of No Return

D. I. JONES

As the heavy bombers roared overhead and disappeared in a south-easterly direction, Luftwaffe night fighter crews departed thankfully for an early supper. By flying low the RAF aircraft were successful in evading radar detection, thus preventing interruption by German fighters. Eventually, however, the bombers must re-appear over central France as they flew back to England. Messerschmitt 110 and Junkers 88 night fighters would be airborne and waiting for their victims to arrive on the scene – hence it looked like being a busy and successful night for the Luftwaffe; just cause for its members to rejoice. Only later did the German aircrews' cheerful mood change to frustrated bitterness as, with fuel running low, they landed after many hours of fruitless patrol. Not only had the RAF bombers failed to turn up, but all trace of them had been lost. It seemed as if they had been swallowed up in the darkness of the velvet sky.

This unusual raid began for me on June 16th, 1943, when I was a member of 97 Squadron, 8 (PFF) Group, stationed at Bourn in Cambridgeshire. Four crews – those of 'Rod' Rodley, Johnny Sauvage, Jimmy Munro and myself – were detailed to fly to Scampton, in 5 Group, as soon as possible. Apparently four target marking crews were required for a special operation. We lost no time in taking off and making our way northwards and, whilst circling Scampton in my Lancaster T-Tommy, I noted that the airfield was completely grass-covered – a fact which was to cause a little anxiety during our stay.

We were made very welcome in the officers' mess despite the friendly rivalry which existed between 5 and 8 Groups, but Group Captain L C Slee, DSO, who was in charge of this special effort demanding our presence, lost no time in acquainting us with the nature of our task. It was to bomb the old Zeppelin sheds at Friedrichshaven on the shores of Lake Constance, where *Wurzburg* radar sets were being made in quantity. The factory was vital to the Germans in their efforts to build up a good stock of this highly desirable war aid. Attacking the factory, however, would be no easy matter. Intelligence insisted that the raid must be carried out before the end of June, but the distances involved made a return flight impossible during the few dark hours of early summer. To be caught over France at dawn would be suicidal, whilst heavy concentrations of flak over Friedrichshaven, plus swarms of fighters over occupied Europe ruled out any possibility of a daylight operation. In addition to these problems the factory was small, necessitating pinpoint target marking and bombing under the worst possible conditions.

Group Captain Slee was cheerful as he outlined these difficulties, but we could find no reason to share in his good humour! Not, that is, until his carefully thought-out plan was unfolded. He asked us to work out our own tactics and loads of flares and TI's for the attack; Rod and Johnny, the veterans of our little group, were not lacking in bright ideas. Intensive bombing and tactical exercises occupied the next two days, during which we theoretically left Cardington's airship sheds a mass of smoking ruins. A severe censorship was imposed on all letters going to and from Scampton. Other airfields interested in the impending raid carried out similar security precautions. An order was issued on June 19th confining all personnel to camp, and on the following day air crews were called to a general briefing. Rumours which had been rife at Scampton as a result of the recent security clampdown were squashed as Group Captain Slee gave information about our target and the method of attack. The operation was to be carried out that same night by 56 Lancasters from 5 Group, plus our four PFF aircraft.

That was a pleasantly calm early summer evening on June 20th 1943 – until the bird songs around Scampton were harshly drowned by the stuttering roar of over 100 Merlin engines starting up. From my seat in the cockpit of T-Tommy I glanced over at the Lancasters of Rod, Johnny and Jimmy. Were they thinking, as I was, of the grass-covered 'runways' we were shortly to use for the take-off? Our aircraft carried a maximum of 2,154 gallons of petrol, plus a heavy load of flares and target markers. All very essential in order to complete the night's work. Unfortunately our Lancs were over-loaded by 2,000 pounds, which meant that using an uneven grass airfield would doubtless be dicey. As I halted opposite the caravan a green light stabbed from its window. A quick final check – flaps down 25 degrees – and T-Tommy trundled forward and swung round into wind. I clamped the brakes full on and, with the control column hard back against my chest, slowly opened the throttles to plus-two pounds of boost. With a hiss of escaping air my left hand relaxed on the brake lever. We moved over the grass, gaining speed over the bumpy surface, and rising gradually as the boundary fence drew disconcertingly close to the Lancaster's blunt nose.

Once across the Channel we dived down to hug the ground over France; tactics designed to keep us below the range of radar scanners. We were now flying in total blackness. A shapeless mass down in the nose of my Lancaster was Tommy Hodkinson, a bomb aimer with remarkably good night vision, who

was searching for the narrow ribbon of the Rhine, and soon found his pinpoint. A steady climb was then made to the pre-arranged bombing height of 5,000 feet. I knew that the 5 Group aircraft would continue on up to 10,000 feet in order to provide an effective cover over the target while we did our job of marking. Tommy announced the approach of Lake Constance and I could see its water gleaming luminously in the darkness. Jimmy Munro and I were to drop a line of flares stretching from Friedrichshaven town to the old Zeppelin works, so that Rod and Johnny could place green and red target markers on the sheds. Jimmy and I would then drop more target markers as required in order to keep the pot boiling.

I turned to port over the lake at zero hour minus three minutes, heading for the dark town and hoping that Jimmy was on schedule; accurate timing was essential to this op. Tommy ordered 'Bomb doors open' just as a string of yellow balls blossomed over to starboard – Jimmy was there. After releasing our flares we swung away, waiting for Rod and Johnny to do their stuff. The defences were active, and the whole of the target area besides being brightly illuminated by our flares was alive with searchlight beams and angry pinpoints of flak. I was perspiring profusely after fighting to hold T-Tommy straight and level on her run up to the target through the concussions of shell bursts.

Over the R/T came the voice of Wing Commander G L Gomm, who took over as Master of Ceremonies when Group Captain Slee developed engine trouble. He very wisely ordered all aircraft to climb a further 5,000 feet in order to avoid possibly heavy casualties. However, the visual marking of our target would have been well nigh impossible from 10,000 feet, and I decided to remain at my original height; a decision also reached by my three PFF colleagues. Naturally this meant that our four aircraft stood out alone in the dark sky, and we promptly received more than our fair share of attention from the defences. Rod Rodley turned over Lake Constance, heading directly between our rows of flares and straining every nerve to drop a target marker before Johnny could make it. He hardly noticed the flak, automatically controlling his Lancaster as she bucketed through the streams of glowing tracer. The factory was plainly visible when Rod opened his bomb doors. His bomb aimer released a target marker, only to see a green cascade burst slightly ahead on the shed roofs – Johnny had beaten him to it after all. Rod then became aware for the first time of the intense hostile defences, but nevertheless swung back to release more target markers. I followed suit.

Within seconds high explosive bombs from the 5 Group aircraft high above came crashing down to our markers. Concussions from the resulting explosions added to our discomfort and I had to abandon one run in to the target because it was impossible to hold T-Tommy on an even keel. Obviously our objective was being well and truly hammered, a fact verified by the angry flames spreading amongst the factory buildings below. During one of five successful runs over the target our aircraft was coned by the searchlights and there followed an apprehensive period when shrapnel rattled along the fuselage like hail stones – until by diving at near-maximum speed we escaped into friendly darkness. Poor Jack Hannah, my wireless operator, stationed at the astro-dome on the lookout for enemy fighters, protested in vigorous terms as he was tossed about like a pea in a pod. Soon our target markers were obscured by drifting dense smoke which covered the radar factory. 5 Group then adopted their alternative method of attack, making timed runs from a prominent landmark on Lake Constance which we illuminated with flares. Their subsequent bombing was remarkably accurate.

Eventually it was time to leave the target, and a course to steer was given by Jimmy, my dour and utterly reliable Scots navigator. A heading north of west would lead us back to base in England, but we turned south towards North Africa. Algeria had recently been taken over by the Allied armies, and Group Captain Slee made full use of this

Left: HAMBURG BY NIGHT – a bomber's view during a night attack on January 30th, 1943. Silhouetted against a pattern of weaving searchlights, bursting flak and exploding bombs, a Lancaster weaves its way out of the danger zone. /Imperial War Museum

Below left: TURIN PATTERNS – a fantasy of searchlights and TI illuminators produced this photo over the Italian target on the night of 12/13th July, 1943 for Flt Sgt Baker in a 97 Squadron Lancaster.

Below: CALAIS CLOBBERED. A day raid on September 25th, 1944 by (among others) the Lancasters of 635 Squadron, PFF.

Right: M-MIKE RETURNS. Lancaster B1, R5626 of 83 Squadron landing at Scampton, prior to the unit's transfer to the PFF at Wyton. 'Mike' eventually completed 23 operations but was lost on its 24th sortie on April 3rd/4th, 1943.

Below: LET-DOWN – the bird comes home to roost. A Lancaster on its final approach – the end of hours of tension, fear and exhaustion . . ./*Flight International*

state of affairs when planning this operation. Instead of returning over a long stretch of enemy-occupied territory to run the gauntlet of night fighters undoubtedly waiting impatiently for us to appear, 60 Lancasters climbed hard for the Alps. A long and peaceful descent over the Italian plain and the Mediterranean culminated in landings at Maison Blanche and Blida airfields in the early dawn. To be precise, 59 Lancasters had an uneventful trip to North Africa. For Rod Rodley the night's incidents were not yet over. As he slowly descended over the Mediterranean, his altimeter needle flickering below the 2,000 feet level, a lurid red glow suddenly blossomed below his Lancaster. Cursing violently, Rod took harsh evasive action to avoid the assumed night fighter or convoy which had disturbed his meditative mood – and, incidentally, had caused him to upset a long-awaited cup of coffee. His flight engineer, Duffy, set off on a tour of inspection of the aircraft, and found the bomb bay a mass of flames, originating from a target marker which had failed to release over target and had ignited when its barometric pressure fuze operated at the pre-set altitude. Rod pulled the bomb jettison toggle and was vastly relieved to see the deadly fireball drop away into the sea below.

Heavy morning mist made our landing at Maison Blanche pretty tricky, but all air crews loudly voiced their praises of an American flying control officer who very efficiently guided in his visiting flock. After three days of sight-seeing in Algiers we returned to England – bombing Spezia, Italy en route for good measure. Jimmy Munro and I were the only Path Finders available to mark this target, for Johnny Sauvage's Lancaster was damaged beyond repair by flak, whilst Rod's badly scorched aircraft needed a great deal of attention. Their two crews stayed on at Maison Blanche and eventually flew home in Rod's machine, via Gibraltar. Our raid on Friedrichshaven radar factory could have resulted in heavy casualties to our relatively small force. By his ingenious tactics, Group Captain Slee achieved his aim of a target badly shattered, at a cost of one aircraft 'lost' and, most important, all air crews safe. It was, to put it mildly, a good show.

'The Beetle wheels its droning flight . . .' – Gray's Elegy personified by a Stirling as it returns at dawn to base; safely 'arrived' . . .

Journey's End

Reaching a target, bombing, and then evading the immediate dangers of flak, searchlight and night fighter, were only half the task for a bomber crew. The journey home was equally fraught with peril: a long slog across hostile territory with diminishing fuel and more often than not a host of problems resulting from damage inflicted on their aircraft during those vital minutes above the objective. Ever prey to radar-directed night fighters, a crew could never afford a moment's relaxation in alertness, despite the all-too human tendency to do just that. The myriad stories of crews who brought back crippled aircraft rather than abandon them for a comparatively safer destiny as a prisoner of war speak volumes for the determination and resolution of the bomber men. Stark evidence of that determination was the scene at many airfields almost nightly, when the bombers finally landed – or attempted to land. Chief witnesses to a host of tragedies were the flying control duty crews – men whose job it was to bring their 'chicks' home as safely as possible. To accomplish this meant a cool head; professional skill of the highest order; an ability to make decisions within seconds without reference to 'higher authority'. And each decision bore responsibility for life or death. Probably no better example of such recurring situations can be given than the following verbatim extracts from the log of Flight Lieutenant A K Halsey, flying control officer at Graveley airfield on the night of

May 4/5th, 1943. Graveley was the first operational airfield to have FIDO installed – the burning petrol pipe-line which bordered a main runway to disperse fog in the immediate area of the landing strip – but on this night the FIDO installation was not yet fully operational. The log notes cover the continuing tale of 'incidents' over a 12-hour period of duty; they also tell a grim story of exhausted crews summoning their last reserves of energy in attempting to come 'home' – many for the last time.

Log Entries:

2055. Ops stated that AOC requires FIDO crew standing by.

2101. Oxford RPM landed from Duxford.

2101. Endeavoured contact F/O Bottom and F/S Beattie without success. W/Cdr Dean gave authority to Tannoy for them.

2102. Tannoy broadcast for F/O Bottom and F/S Beattie.

2111. Oxford RPM took off for Duxford.

2120. F/O Bottom reported FIDO crew standing by.

2130. Ops state our aircraft have as an alternative station – Wrexham.

2245. Ops state alternative station is High Ercall instead of Wrexham.

0214. Vesta Q calling Darky, was answered, requested permission to land.

0219. Wellington (Vesta Q) landed on 04 runway. Base (Wing) informed.

SALVAGE PARTY. Hoisting the wreck of Lancaster T-Tilly onto bogies to remove it from the runway after a wheels-up crash landing. 'Tilly' – Lanc BI, R5845, served with 97 Squadron; was then used by 1660 Heavy Conversion Unit; and was eventually struck off RAF charge in September 1945./*Keystone Press Agency*

A/C	Captains	Etd	Off	Eta	Landed	Remarks
U	Sgt Andrews	2202	2203	0246	0433	—
Q	Sgt Wright	2203	2205	0246	0416	Landed on grass parallel with runway, crossed FIDO.
M	Sgt Hall	2204	2206	0246	0259	—
Y	F/Sgt Cobb	2205	2207	0246		Crashed at Toseland @ abt 0409, all crew except rear gunner killed.
C	W/O Lee	2206	2211	0246	0507	Landed at Oulton.
E	Sgt Williams	2207	2209	0246		Crew baled out. Crashed at Barton Seagrave, short petrol.
K	F/L Cranswick	2224	2220	0246	0413	Short of petrol. 0251 QDM 227dgs Stn D/F.
R	P/O Hickson	2225	2225	0246	0040	BBA Pulham 2357. Fix 1st 01 Pulham 5222N 0200E @ 2354 Ident.

0245. Wyton reported HA flying S from Norwich.

0259. M/35 landed on 04 runway.

0252. Wyton reported HA 10 mls E of them, flying SW.

0255. Air Raid Purple.

0300. A/405 landed without previous communication with Control. A/c overshot and crashed through fence and across the Graveley rd. Ambulance sent to render assistance. A/c previously shot up, two wounded. No brake pressure or R/T.

0315. Vis from Met 3,000 yds.

0322. Instructions given to change runway to 25 as A/405 was reported to be obstructing end of 04. A/c were not landed on it until AOP was in position owing to the danger of two A/c landing at once, as R/T communication was very bad, and several A/c more in distress.

0323. Air Raid White.

0323. Met reported vis 1,200 yds, meanwhile F/83 was overhead on two engines. B/405 on three engines. S/405 short of petrol.

0323. Q/35 u/c stuck down and A/c overheating. K/35 short of petrol.

0330. S/405 landed on 25 with contact strip.

0350. F/83 landed on two engines on 25

SOME WERE LUCKY ... Lancaster 'HMT River Spey' of 83 Squadron which was 'bent' on landing, but the crew survived . . ./*Wg Cdr R P Elliott*, DSO, DFC

and became stuck at end of runway. F's R/T was very bad and could not receive any of our transmissions. Greens were flashed to him repeatedly giving his A/c letter.

0352. Changed onto 04 runway while nature of obstruction on 25 by F was investigated.

0400. Maybug B called asking if we were receiving, we replied several times and then asked if he was receiving us, received no reply.

0405. Y/35 was given permission to land.

0408. Tried to contact Maybug B, W/405 and T/405 who had previously been given heights to fly, with a view to diverting them, but were unable to establish contact.

0409. Y/35 crashed after hitting tree about half a mile W of crossing of Toseland-Yelling road and Graveley to Croxton road. ACP stated later that A/c appeared to approach too far E. This crash was not reported until 0515.

0410. B/405 landed on 04 runway without permission and was mistaken for Y. B became stuck on E.FIDO gates N of main runway with tail on 04 runway. Another A/c reported stuck at intersection of 25 and 36. Flight crash party sent to render assistance.

0413. K/35 landed on 04 runway. He was landed out of turn as he had only 15 mins petrol left.

0414. Q/35 given priority landing instructions as his u/c was stuck down and he was over-heating.

0416. Q/35 landed.

0420. Called E/35 and C/35 and told them to divert to Oulton 065 dgs, 70 mls. A/c had difficulty in receiving owing to bad interference on R/T. After several repetitions E said he had in-

sufficient endurance. C did not acknowledge receipt of instructions and E was told to stand by. Meanwhile U/35 who had asked several times if he could attempt a landing, was given permission to land. Station D/F instructed to pass message on W/T to divert C and E.

0433. U/35 landed on 04 runway.

0435. E/35 given permission to land. He made two attempts to land on 14, then the runway was changed to 25 with contact strip and sodium lights. E was informed of this on R/T and acknowledged receipt of message. E did not make an attempt to land on 25 but disappeared and became out of R/T touch. He was called repeatedly without success.

0507. C/35 landed at Oulton.

0515. RAF Regt reported an A/c had crashed at Toseland.

0521. PC Lewis of Yelling Police reported crash at Toseland.

0522. Informed by Cpl Crossley that our spare crash tender is u/s. On W/Cdr Dean's authority sent Control crash tender, MO and ambulance to scene of crash.

0530. ACP reported E/35 was last observed by him to be climbing and flying in W direction @ 2/3,000 ft.

0600. Chelveston reported two of crew of E/35 had baled out and had been picked up. Arranged to send transport to collect them.

0600. Crash tender reported Y/35 had crashed into a pond and was partly burned and had set fire to a haystack. Crash party put out the fire in conjunction with the AFS.

0630. MO reported Y/35 badly smashed up, six of crew killed but tail gunner

Left: . . . AND SOME WERE NOT. Grim reminder of the added dangers of bombing en masse over a target. A Lancaster which had its rear turret, and gunner, completely chopped off by a bomb from another Lancaster above. The severed ammunition tracks are still visible.

Below: An 83 Squadron Lancaster which not only lost its rear turret but had its hydraulics system ruptured, and had to belly-land at base eventually.

who escaped serious injury stated that on approaching to land A/c hit a tree.

0700. Teleg received from Cpl Wisson, RAF Police – 'Sgt Tucker baled out of RAF A/c attached RAF Graveley. Second out of plane.'

0700. Arranged for transport to collect members of crew from Chelveston, and then proceed to Trimwood for Sgt Tucker.

0725. FIDO crew stood down on authority of PFF.

0730. Ops reported that Chelveston had now located six members of crew of E/35.

0815. Commissioner of Kettering Police said F/Sgt Brown was picked up at Raunds, and another at Kinstead, and both were sent to Chelveston. A/c had crashed at Barton Seagrave and is being taken over by Grafton Underwood.

0820. RAF Grafton Underwood phoned saying that they were effecting crash procedure and that Sgt Williams, the pilot of E/35, was in the vicinity of the A/c.

0910. Chelveston phoned saying they had four memberw of crew and were awaiting remaining two who were understood to be in vicinity.

0915. B/405 removed from 04 runway, but

25 runway still obstructed by F/83.

0930. Runway 25 clear.

Official observations re-landings

(1) At ETA of A/c conditions here were good. Vis being 3,000 yds or more, no cloud, and wind right on 04 runway at 5/10mph. There was therefore no reason to change to main runway or to light FIDO. As we were fit we were asked to take some A/c from Gransden and Wyton.

(2) At 0323 Met reported vis 1,200yds and by this time five distressed A/c overhead. The wind was still NNE at 5/10. It was considered more expedient to endeavour to land these A/c forthwith rather than delay to light FIDO. FIDO would have taken some time to come into action, would have created an amount of smoke and, in view of the actual surface wind strength, would possibly have caused a considerable increase in strength of surface wind; so that A/c landing on FIDO would have landed partly down-wind and with considerable port drift. The Met gradient wind at the time was NNE at 10/15mph.

(3) Meanwhile, at 0330, S/405 landed on 25 and at 0350 F/83 landed on 25. The latter proceeded along 25 and became stuck. This necessitated investigation and to save delay in landing, the runway was changed back to 04. Again FIDO was considered, but in view of obstruction by F/83 was considered impracticable.

Below: BULLS-EYE. Cannon shell holes which 'ventilated' one bomber over Berlin. The 12-inch ruler provides a scale for size.

Right: Two views of flak damage to B-Baker, a Lancaster of 35 Squadron on the morning of February 8th, 1945.

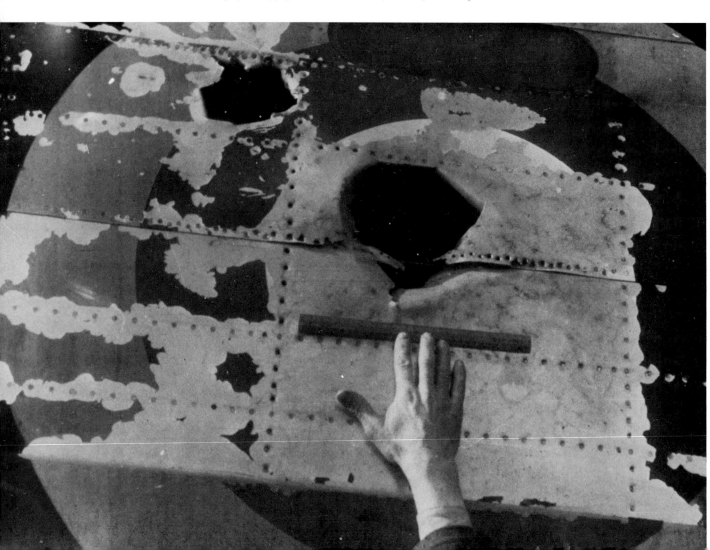

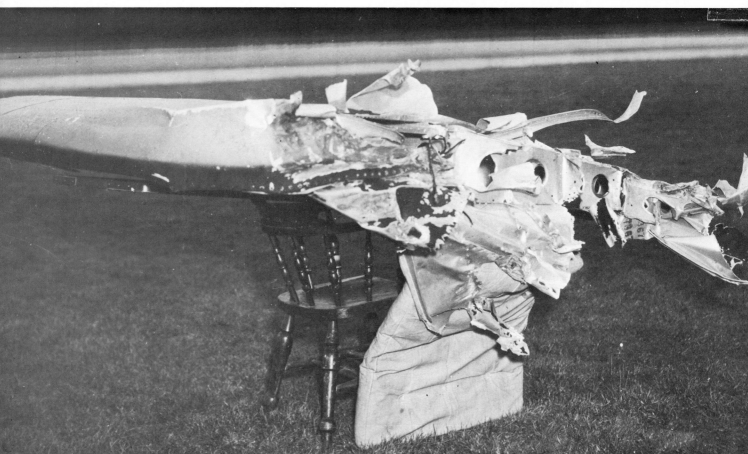

(4) Four A/c then landed on 04, meanwhile a further obstruction by an A/c at the intersection of 25 and 36 was reported, again rendering FIDO impracticable.

(5) Eventually the last mentioned obstruction was reported to be clear and F/83 reported be at the extreme end of 25. E had made two attempts to land on 04 and he was then told to land on 25 and all available lighting was put on for him. E acknowledged instructions to land on 25. At this stage FIDO could have been lit but it would have caused more delay and smoke. E was short of petrol so FIDO was not lit, so that E could come in on 25 straight away. E however did not attempt this and was reported by ACP to be climbing to 2/3,000 ft and flying westwards. Endeavour was made to re-establish R/T communication with him but without success.

Demi-official observations re-landings:

(1) Considerable speeding up of landings could have been effected if we had had a control van fitted with R/T. Obstructing A/c could have been located and assessed immediately and the next A/c landed by R/T from the van. As it was, we had to wait for reports to come in from various sources.

(2) Marshalling presented some complications. The diverted A/c came at a moment's notice, and it took well over half an hour for the Duty Crew to report, as they had to be fetched out of bed by a runner. Diverted A/c were landing and had to be marshalled by the Airman of the Watch and Control trainee. The services of these two men were thus lost to the Control Room at the time they were most urgently needed to answer countless telephone calls. It is suggested that the Duty Crew sleep at a flight dispersal hut on all nights, where they can be contacted by telephone at a moment's notice, whether operations are in progress from this Station or not.

(3) R/T was bad. This was probably the result of several A/c overhead trying to transmit at the same time. Reports have since been received that parts of our transmissions were clear, but that half-way through they were jammed by other transmissions. This caused considerable delay in passing instructions owing to the necessity of numerous repetitions. It is considered that a contributory factor to the delay was unnecessary transmissions from A/c asking their turn to land etc after they had been given heights to fly.

(4) It is imperative that we have Angle of Glide Indicators provided for each runway in order to avoid the delay which must take place, equipped as we are with only two, when runways have to be changed in an emergency.

Left: Just some of the damage caused to Lancaster ND875 of 156 Squadron on the night of February 7/8th, 1945, when its skipper, Sqn Ldr A W G Cochrane, DSO, DFC, was master bomber for a raid on Goch. Early in the raid he collided with another Lancaster, but continued his job until forced to return. Cochrane, from Rawene, New Zealand, flew more than 80 sorties; 48 of them on PFF sorties, and 14 of these as a master bomber.

Above NACHTJAGER. A Messerschmitt Bf 110 G-4 night fighter, fitted with Lichtenstein radar in its nose./*Bundesarchiv*

Left/above: FLAK – the most-used anti-aircraft gun was the 8.8 cm 'Flak 36', requiring (ideally) a ten-man team to operate. Controlling a four-gun battery was a predictor, which provided the gun crews with azimuth, elevation and fuse-setting data. Predicted flak was most feared by crews during the unswerving bombing run needed for precision bombing or marking a target./*Archiv Schliephake*

Far left: Mid-air collision occurred often during the many concentrated raids of the war's latter years. Though not a PFF aircraft, this Halifax (MZ465, MH-Y, 51 Sqn) had about nine feet of its nose section chopped away in an aerial collision over Saarbrucken on the night of January 13/14th, 1945. Its skipper, Fg Off A L Wilson, lost his navigator and bomb aimer, both of whom were in the nose at the moment of impact. With only three instruments on his dashboard working, Wilson brought the Halifax back; and is seen here (centre) next morning with the crew survivors.

Below: OPS COMPLETED. The operations board at PFF headquarters after raids during the night of April 4/5th, 1945. Nos 1, 3, 4, 6 and 8 Groups participated in raids against Hamburg, Leuna, Lutzkendorf, Magdeburg and Berlin – the latter two being the PFF's objectives that night.

Mating tail units to 1,000lb and 500lb MC HE bombs at dispersal – a unusual procedure from the normal where complete bombs, tails fitted, and fused, were ordinarily delivered from the bomb dump.

Rex Benson was a bomber crew member from the earliest days of the war, and by 1943 was a Squadron Leader flying a mahogany bomber (i.e. had a desk job) at his Group HQ, but itching to return to operations; having completed 32 operational sorties previously. The following extracts from his unpublished autobiography are of exceptional interest, describing not only various incidents of his PFF tour, but also giving a brief glimpse into some off-duty events and personalities.

In the autumn of 1943 the 'body-snatcher' of the Path Finder Force gave a lecture at HQ on the latest developments in the bombing offensive, and I felt way out of date. He was Wing Commander 'Hamish' Mahaddie, who had been an NCO at the start of the war on Whitleys, an ex-Halton entrant, and one of the few pilots trained for night bombing. He was a veteran of the early leaflet raids on Vienna, when most rear gunners were frost-bitten achieving absolutely nothing worthwhile. Hamish had collected a string of 'gongs', being one of the original Path Finders, and was an excellent raconteur, speaking in an understandable Scots tongue. He could have sold calliopes to Red Indians and refrigerators to the Eskimos; he certainly 'sold' PFF, as the Force was known, to me. I sought him out afterwards and asked him for a berth. 'Aye, laddie', he said, and took a note of my name; this sort of thing being the sole purpose of his trip, to gain volunteers, and experienced Observers, trained in both navigation and bombing, were No 1 priority. I decided to pay a call on the PFF, properly known as 8 Group, and chose Wyton, near their HQ at Hunting-

don. Many were the familiar faces, all with extra 'rings' like myself, but with (medal) ribbons which I did not possess. I felt like an outcast, as though I had walked into an exclusive club of which I was not a member.

I played bridge in the mess and it seemed to be still early in the proceedings when two officers strolled in, in flying rig and armed with pots of beer. This could mean only one thing – they had just returned from a raid. One was Flight Lieutenant 'Stan' Baldwin, then nearing his century of ops, and they had returned from Berlin in a Mosquito. I was astounded, and now the bug was biting me. I was sure that because we fed crews to 1 Group I would be then be posted to 156 Squadron, which had come to PFF from 1 Group originally. They were based at Warboys, close to Wyton, but I was very disappointed with the site, a feeling due in part to the heavy rain that fell all the time that I was there. It was very dispersed with none of the amenities of Wyton, where the living was equal to Marham. The living quarters were a long way from the Mess and called for a walk across muddy fields, or a longer walk by country lane. Worse still, the aerodrome was even further away, in the opposite direction. I arrived back at Eggington Hall, the Group HQ, not quite as enthusiastic as I had been the previous night at Wyton. I fully expected to be appointed as the Squadron Bombing Leader when the present one, an ex-jockey named F------, was due to be killed; so when I was at Wyton I arranged to be tested for my powers of night vision by a special device rigged up by 'Doc' McGown, a Wing Commander medic who flew occasionally on

SEEING 'EM OFF – the ground crews, male and female, wave a final 'Good Luck' to a Lancaster crew as it gathers momentum on its take-off run. A dusk scene which became a familiar 'routine' at heavy bomber stations.

operations, and actually won a DFC while I was in the Group. I obtained the top score, so had reason to believe that that would clinch it. As it turned out I never used a bomb sight again.

I had felt for some time that I had not much more to offer the Group I was in. Despite all the conferences at High Wycombe and the operational Groups, there was only one sure way to know what was happening over the other side, and that was to be 'with it'. I was making decisions affecting the futures of a great number of air crews, and this should have been the prerogative of an older and wiser man. Within a few days I learnt that I was to be posted. A posting to the Path Finder Force could not be varied, and I was to be released from Group HQ as soon as a replacement had been chosen. Under normal circumstances all senior officers with acting rank, upon posting to another Group, were interviewed beforehand by the Air Officer Commanding, to meet with his approval. This was always waived in the case of 8 Group. They accepted so many in this category and Don Bennett had no time for this kind of desk work; he left the selections to Hamish Mahaddie.

No one went straight to a squadron in PFF – not even squadron commanders – without first going through the PFF Training Unit, which was then at Upwood; another beautiful, cleanly laid out unit on the Marham pattern. The adjoining room to mine was occupied by Group Captain John Searby, who had been the master-bomber on the Peenemunde raid five months previously. He appeared to be there in a supernumerary title, as he was not the station commander, but senior officers in this special force were usually 'held' in some manner, and rarely left to go elsewhere, and there were always vacancies to fill. I was soon to cease wondering at the number of 'rings' that abounded wherever I looked.

Being still under the impression that I was to be a visual bomb aimer – having done three courses at Manby, nearly three years as an instructor and staff officer in this capacity – I expected to be given training as such, and in the modern gadgets that I had not met. Among these was the Air Position Indicator (API), which kept a plot of the course flown, even if it was like a corkscrew. To me this was a wonderful innovation, as on my first tour there was no way of knowing where one had been heading when spiralling and twisting to avoid being coned. The next piece of equipment to cause me to open my eyes was the H2S – the 'gen box' – which gave a radar view of the ground. This showed up the coastline and built-up areas if used skilfully. Thick cloud made no difference, so there was to be no more great reliance on visual pin-points. I

was looking forward to instruction in the use of this, as bomb aiming was not always visual, in fact rather the exception, and bombs were often dropped above cloud with the aid of the 'box'. The third item was a Distant Reading (DR) Compass, which made the old type mounted in a bowl seem like a sun dial compared with a clock.

After a few hours of looking around, seeing an old familiar face here and there, I was astonished to be told by the Chief Ground Instructor, Squadron Leader Bob Scrivener, that I was to be a navigator! I felt as though I had called into the dressing room of a team at Wembley to wish them luck, and been told that I was to play in goal. The efficiency and fame of the PFF depended in the main on the superior skill shown by the navigators, who not only had to locate a target, but *had* to arrive on the dot. I realised that in putting me up for this, Scrivener was raising my stock, but I was right out of touch. I did two 'dry swims', which were the usual exercises done without leaving the ground, and this took me

Top: A pall of smoke rising from burning Karlsruhe; with TI's cascading at top left, adding to the 'brew-up' below.

Above: MAIN STREAM – the massive formation of main force bombers which became a common sight in 1944-45. In this view, at least 85 Lancasters may be identified.

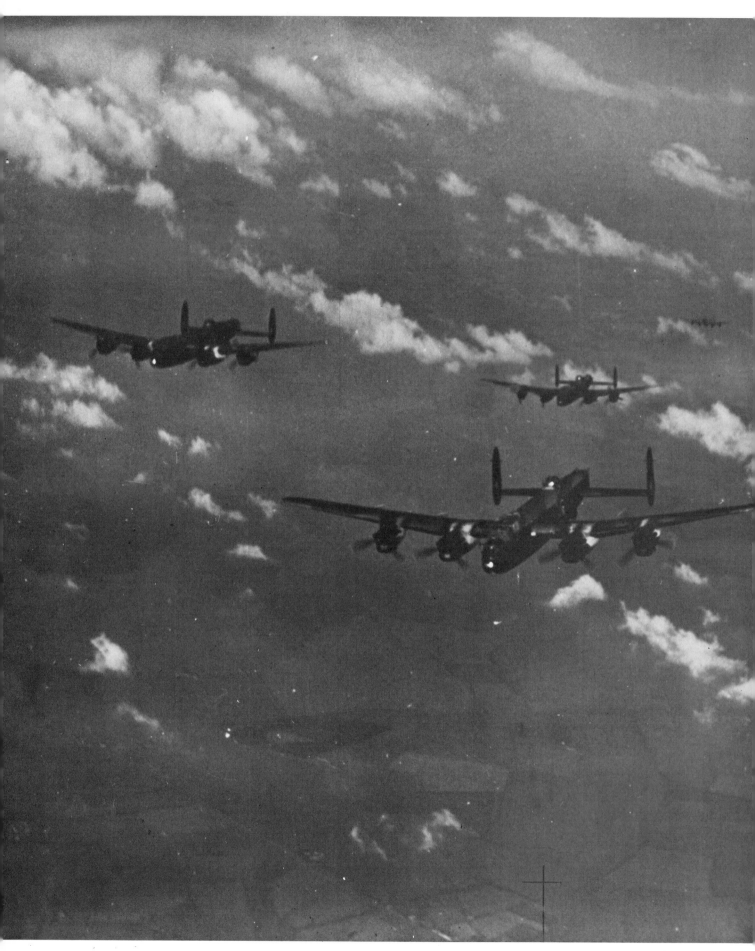

right back to the 1940 days at Harwell. To me the results seemed appalling; I could not get the hang of arriving at a certain point 600 miles away at an exact time, and was now more certain that I would be behind a bomb sight. It mattered little, and my plotting charts were mysteriously 'mislaid'. I received high marks for keenness, and an assessment for ability that could have meant anything; there was a remark that I was 'out of practice'! I was on the unit for four days only, but in that time I joined a crew that had been cooling their heels for a considerable time, awaiting a navigator. Like myself, they had come to the unit as individuals, and were strangers to one another.

To make matters worse (as I thought then, but was to be pleasantly mistaken later), my set operator who was to work the H2S and obtain fixes for me, had never flown operationally. The pilot, Squadron Leader Tom Godfrey, already had a DFC for landing successfully in the drink; the rear gunner, Flying Officer Billy Bramwell, a grocer's assistant from the North, had a DFM for shooting down two Jerries; and the W/Op, Flying Officer Jenkins, had a DFM from my last squadron – so there was plenty of experience in the right places. The flight engineer had flown for a few hours only, and was very raw, but I had to admire his spirit in volunteering for PFF with nothing under his belt but guts. The mid-upper gunner, Flight Lieutenant Hinds, was an unknown quantity, and gave the impression that he'd been on several 'shaky do's', as indeed he had. So I went to war again, but could not have arrived at Warboys at a worse time. 156 Squadron had lost 14 crews in the previous three nights, and had been ordered not to fly on that night (January 27th, 1944) when all the other squadrons were going to Berlin – an unusual circumstance. Those 14 crews represented about 100 men, and instead of ops there was a 'wake', and it was reminiscent of the 1914-18 RFC parties in France, when everyone was expected to become sozzled and forget. The RAF was right on the ball in this respect; it was the appropriate occasion to play jolly and lively music, such as 'Goodbye Dolly Gray' on returning from a funeral, however much we had slow-marched in step with a dirge on the way to the grave.

The first casualties came in the apple race. All Mess chairs were placed in two rows, backs facing inwards, to form a wide lane straight down the room. At the far end were two buckets of water, each containing an apple on the top, and the rules were simple. There were two contestants, and each had to stand with his forehead on a stick about three feet long; then to be turned round and round fairly quickly until he was hopelessly giddy.

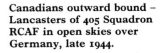

Canadians outward bound – Lancasters of 405 Squadron RCAF in open skies over Germany, late 1944.

Each was then released to make his way to the bucket and retrieve the apple in his teeth – first one to withdraw it being the winner. There was an element of variety introduced. If the contestants were both spun inwardly they tended to meet head-on with a sickening thud after a few yards, and the bodies were removed as though they had been gladiators in the arena who had received a 'thumbs down' sign. If spun the other way, they crashed into the chairs, and made their way by a series of collisions, like a runaway car bouncing along a row of parked cars. This lively game was stopped when it seemed that we would run out of contestants. and not be able to put anyone into the air for a while. The next item was to put our bare feet into a tarry mess and leave their impression on the ceiling; this was dangerous enough for an acrobat without a safety wire, but somehow we managed it. Beer was drunk from a common utensil, the limit being two fingers per man per drink, which was quite a lot of beer from a bucket.

Then came the individual contests. Group Captain 'Ginger' Eaton, the squadron commander, was placed on a table with his heels just over the end; his assistants slowly tipped it up, with his head hanging downwards. He appeared to grip tightly with his heels, and I was admiring the manner in which he seemed to hang, without using his hands, in an almost vertical position. 'What about the new squadron leader?', chuckled 'Fatty' Collings, the Station Commander; a former captain of the British bobsleigh team. Anything that Eaton can do, I can do better. I thought, and took up the challenge – I'd show these buggers a thing or two! It was a terrible strain on my feet, and the skin felt as if it was being scraped off just above the heels – which wasn't surprising because it was. Then I heard someone say, 'Hold it at 40 degrees.' I thought, 'Hell, am I only up that far?' as the table edge bit into my tendons. There was no intention of allowing me to go any further, as at that very moment I received the contents of a pint pot of beer down each trouser leg – and this was in January! Eaton had not held on at all, but had been unobtrusively supported, as a gag for which I had fallen. I was obliged to stand with my back to the fire in an attempt to dry myself out. While so doing, Squadron Leader Thomas, the squadron navigation officer, was engaged in showing his skill at guessing weights. He was picking up officers of all shapes and sizes, including 'Fatty', and certainly estimating with a great deal of accuracy. I was the next to be picked up. Thomas lingered for a while holding me, then said finally, 'Twelve-Two'. He was not far out in his estimate, but as he was about to sit me back on the table, I heard a faint scraping sound. I hurriedly thrust my hands underneath my rump and was just in time to avoid sitting in a deep tray of stale beer. I did not get any wetter, but Flight Lieutenant 'Dixie' Dean, who had failed to slide the tray quietly enough, had to sit in it himself for 'spoiling the fun.' Despite 'High Cockalorum', with very senior officers being sent hurtling to the floor by mere pilot-officers wetting their new 'ring' for the first time, there was little physical damage; no bones were broken, but there were many thick heads, mostly as a result of the beer which, although we reckoned it only to be 'gnat's', was drunk in great quantities. Next day we returned to normal, fully operational, with rank coming back into its own, as though the levelling-up process of the night before had not happened.

Within a few days our new crew was blooded, after one night cross-country which I cocked up, as did nearly everyone else. It had been laid on as an exercise, and the others cocked it up for devilment, thinking it a waste of time. Appropriately enough, the op was to Berlin where, we had been advised at briefing, every bomb there counted as two bombs elsewhere. Later I was to hear this said about Munich and Nuremberg. We went as a 'Supporter' crew – the role given always to new crews in PFF. A saturation bombing raid of this nature lasted about 30 minutes, which meant in theory that a plane arrived over the target with about the same frequency as a tube train would arrive at the platform at Piccadilly. The Path Finders marked the target first, and so that they could escape the

The stream from above – a section of Lancasters going over in daylight on July 19th, 1944; viewed from 18,000 ft.

full attention of the fighters and ground defences, it was necessary for other, less 'important' aircraft to keep them company; the only ones being relied upon to do so were other Path Finders, hence the role of Supporter. It was vital to be on time, otherwise the markers stood a risk of being picked off. Our time to bomb was 21.13 hours on the evening of February 15th. At one time our chances of doing this seemed as remote as to appear impossible. On the way across the North Sea our GEE set became unserviceable; a newer aid to navigation, easy to operate (I was shown it only the once on the ground), which gave immediate fixes using transits on a time-base, but with a limited range, usually about 100 miles from our coast, due to very effective jamming from the opposition.

I was soon advised by Jenkins that all the other bombers were going to port, and that we were wandering to starboard of the main stream. He was using an anti-fighter device called *Fishpond*, which gave a radar contact of anyone skulking on our tail, and it was clear that we had shaken off all our friends instead, who should have been behind us all the way for we were all given the same course. I was not so vain as to imagine that I was the only one 'in step', but there was nothing I could do about it except not panic, as the set could have been faulty. We were due to make landfall near Stavanger, then fly across the south of Sweden 'by accident.' (This was neutral territory, but their AA guns were always 'jammed' when we did this . . .) The route then lay south from Rostock in an attempt to fool the enemy as to our real objective. It was a very long way round, but the direct route would have been suicide. We went blithely on, and the H2S was still working. Serviceability of the equipment in 8 Group was remarkable; rarely did it fail to function and this was due entirely to the skill of the ground crews. At last the Danish coast came into view on the set, near Sylt. It was as though I was looking at a small atlas, but we knew we were the only British aircraft within miles, being far south of our route. I had to make a quick calculation, and worked out that by continuing on our course we would make Berlin with a few minutes in hand, which I could waste on a dog leg.

Immediately after crossing the coast, and nearing Flensburg, up came Bramwell on the intercomm – he was usually quiet for the entire trip – 'There's a fooking Ju 88 on our tail. I'll give the bastard a squirt if he comes any closer.' This seemed like the promise of action, but almost immediately there followed a string of rich oaths. 'The bugger blew up!' he shouted. It seems that the flak which had been chasing us around to little purpose, had caught the Jerry instead. It was cloudy over

Wing Commander K H 'Bobby' Burns, DSO, DFC, who served in PFF headquarters staff 1944-45.

the target, with what I had come to expect as the usual Berlin cover, but the outline of the city was very clear on the set; even the River Spree could be distinguished, and there was no doubt about where our bombs were going, even though we were bombing on radar. I selected the bombs, fuzed them, and looked at my watch; it was coming up to 21.13 hrs precisely. I gave Cooper the release button, saying, 'OK you can drop 'em'. His face beamed and he pressed the tit so hard that I thought it would break. I heard the familiar jerks from underneath, and we were away as the clouds were beginning to glow red when the bombing intensified. Then the H2S gave up the ghost, and we flew back by dead reckoning. When we were within GEE range we were only 10 miles out, so it turned out to be an easy trip with no real incidents. I had felt the hardened veteran, letting Cooper have the honour. Within a year he was six trips ahead of me, with a Bar to his DFC, but I do not think he derived more satisfaction than when he dropped that first load. I, of course, had fallen down the 'thunderbox' and come up smelling of violets, from the point of view of arriving on the dot; Thomas made no

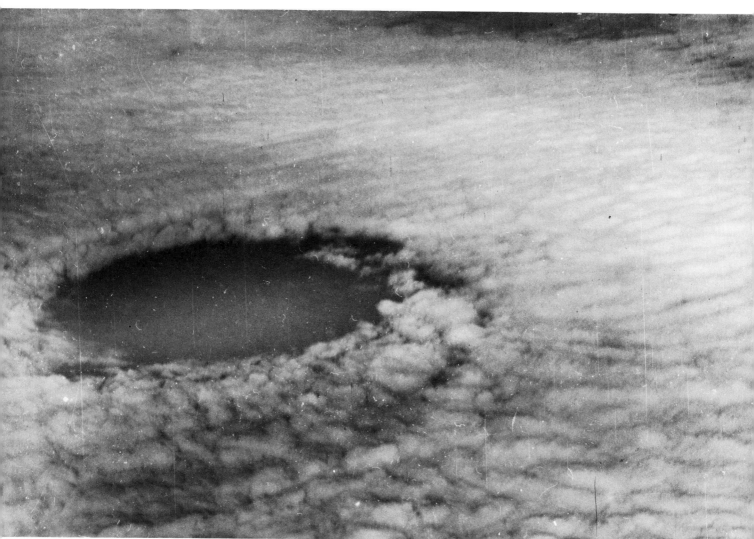

bones about telling me so after looking at my plot.

In all, I completed 34 ops with the PFF, and a variety of people and events remain vivid in my mind. On Sunday, May 31st, 1944, being at a loose end, I took Pilot Officer Taggart, RAAF as Master Bomber to Tergnier, a marshalling yard which we did over so well that he gained a 'gong'. (Can you imagine this sort of arrangement in the Navy – almost a Midshipman-equivalent in charge of a fleet of ships?) On the raid we lost Pilot Officer Samson RAAF and crew. Months later, when I was at Warboys, on August 27th I went to a party at Upwood, and in passing through the billiards room, an officer passed me with a sly grin, and I called out, without thinking, 'Hallo Sammy'. It didn't strike me immediately that it was Samson, back from the chopper. The Reaper had claimed most of his crew but his brolly had worked OK. Instead of making tracks for the UK, he joined up with the Maquis, taking delight in knocking off Jerries from closer range than hitherto. Finally he was made to return.

I was walking to the flight office one morning when an RAAF Flight Sergeant on crutches, with one leg, passed. He put one crutch on his left arm, balanced on one leg, and to my deep embarrassment, saluted me. He was Flight Sergeant G C C Smith of Sydney, and he was soon after given the CGM (Conspicuous Gallantry Medal) for one of the bravest feats on the squadron. It was a Berlin trip on February 15th, 1944, and I had also been on it. He was the only Australian in his crew. He was usually the mid-upper gunner, but on this trip occupied the rear turret. They were attacked by a night fighter on the run-in. Smith shot it down but a cannon shell had shattered his leg, and bullets had hit him elsewhere. His turret was u/s, and the aircraft was in a mess as the mid-upper gunner was out of action, also wounded in the leg but able to be taken out of his turret. Smith, knowing that the other gunner was out of action, refused to leave his turret and operated it manually. On the way back his oxygen mask froze up. By chopping away at the door, Smith was pulled out after an hour; the bits of his leg kept jamming inside. His leg was amputated the next day, and he was frost-bitten.

One night I was responsible for the arrangements for a big Mess party. There were lashings of everything, with smoked salmon flown down from Wick, and I was supposed to limit expenditure to £150, so that Mess profits left over could be snaffled by Air Ministry. I 'miscalculated' to the extent that it eventually cost £750. There was a heap of food, but this was not supposed to be started on until the AOC had arrived. Among it were three beautiful large chickens for display purposes only, all in glace, done up by the master chef at Wyton, where they were to return next day for a Wyton party. Gazing hungrily at the birds were Wing Commander Burns and Squadron Leaders Rodley and Benson, but they were placed deliberately out of reach of such 'gannets'. Burns, a tall man, then unscrewed his false hand (lost over Berlin when he was shot down), and replaced it with a hook. As we held his ankles he was able to reach over to snaffle all three birds – and they were delicious!

A final memory of RAF 'efficiency' concerned the winter of 1944. It was so cold that the 'troops' on 1 Site (of which I was CO) cut all the wood from the fences, so that they fell down when the sheep leaned against them. I carried out a block inspection and found all the wooden luggage racks missing, and when I pulled out the drawers of the chests, they 'came away in me 'and' – no backs! I ordered fuel immediately. In August 1945, when I was about the last person on the base, and about to drive away for the last time – an enormous load of coal was delivered . . .!

Left: BOMBS AWAY – a Lancaster, its bomb bay doors agape, releasing its load through clouds onto a V-1 rocket site on July 27th, 1944.

Below left: The original 'hole in the clouds' for bomb aimers . . .! A natural phenomenon photographed over Germany.

Below: COLOGNE CONCENTRATION. Precision day bombing on the totally ruined cathedral city of Cologne, March 2nd, 1945.

'Queenie'—the Veteran

GATE GUARDIAN.
Lancaster B1, R5868, on display beside the main entrance to RAF Scampton, Lincoln (at back of aircraft) in 1965. Here the aircraft was marked as OL-Q, its original 83 Squadron coding. The 12,000lb & 22,000lb HE bombs displayed under her nose were never capable of being installed in Queenie . . .

To the bomber crews the aircraft in which they flew to war were not merely metal machines but distinct personalities; each one slightly – or greatly – different from any other of the same species. Once aboard and outward bound on an operation the bomber became their exclusive home, transporting and mothering them until the heartfelt moment of relief when its wheels touched the runway on landing back at base, safely arrived. For thousands of men of RAF Bomber Command their aircraft became their hearses; their last tangible connection with the earth they had left behind.

Lancaster B1, R5868 was not only a distinct personality, but one of the very few that achieved more than 100 operational missions. Indeed, it was said of her that the navigators could sleep during any return trip – she 'knew her own way home'. This profound trust in an inanimate object such as a bomber aircraft can be attributed to youthful superstition, adolescent fancy; the fact remains that R5868 always came back, and during nearly three years of war flying only suffered minimal damage to its airframe, with only two minor wounds amongst its many crew members.

Today R5868 is unique in that it is the sole surviving example in Britain of the many thousands of Lancasters which flew operationally with the RAF in World War Two. As such it is a permanent memorial to all Lancaster crews who never came back – and a reminder to future generations of the sacrifices made by the men of Bomber Command who died in battle.

To the contractors and manufacturers Lancaster B1, R5868 was merely one of a batch, serialled R5768-R5917, of Avro Manchesters and Lancasters ordered under Contract No 982866 for delivery to the rapidly expanding RAF Bomber Command between March 1941 and August 1942. Of this batch 43 machines were built as Manchesters and the remainder as Lancasters. Thus R5868 was the 27th Lancaster to come from the factory floor of Metropolitan Vickers at Trafford Park, Manchester, and was delivered to Avro's Woodford base on June 20th, 1942 for final assembly and testing. Nine days later R5868 arrived at RAF Scampton, near Lincoln as the latest replacement aircraft for 83 Squadron, where she was allotted to B Flight and given the code letter 'Q-Queenie'. As such the bomber was initially taken over by Squadron Leader Ray Hilton, DFC, a veteran bomber captain of 83 Squadron, who flew her on several local formation practice flights on July 5th, 6th and 7th. On the night of July 8/9th, Hilton took Queenie on her baptism of operations; one of 10 squadron aircraft participating on a raid against Wilhelmshaven. Her war load was 1,260lb of incendiaries which were duly delivered on the target area from 16,000 feet, and all 83 Squadron's aircraft returned to base without mishap; Queenie touching down at Scampton at 0420 hours on July 9th. Two nights later Ray Hilton took her to Danzig and dropped five 1,000lb high explosive (HE) bombs. There was little incident on the trip apart from some troublesome searchlights near the target which were promptly 'extinguished' by Queenie's gunners.

On July 14/15th Queenie changed her load, and her skipper, when with Pilot Officer J E Partridge at the controls she took off just after 11pm with a full bay of sea mines for a Gardening trip to Bordeaux; depositing them in the Gironde river from 800 feet. Switching to a daylight sortie on July 18th, Ray Hilton set off at 1050 hrs with an HE load, bound for the sprawling Krupps works at Essen. On the outward leg Queenie met her first Luftwaffe opponents when two Focke Wulf 190s approached. In the event neither fighter attacked, and on his return Hilton was awarded a Bar to his DFC; whilst an air gunner, Plt Off A F McQueen received a DFC. Queenie flew nine more operations from Scampton during the following three weeks, including four sorties against Duisburg; and suffered her first flak damage on the night of July 26/27th when Jack Partridge flew Queenie to Hamburg on a fire raid. On August 15th, 1942, 83 Squadron moved en bloc from Scampton to Wyton – one of the founder

Below: Wing Commander Ray Hilton, DSO, DFC, who was the first skipper to fly Queenie on operations, with 83 Squadron at Scampton; and who flew a total of 18 operations at her helm. Hilton was eventually killed on his third tour of operations, on the night of November 23rd, 1943, over Berlin.

Right: Queenie's most-used crew. L-R: Flt Sgt Bill Webster (Flight Engineer); Flt Sgt Len Thomas (Mid-upper air gunner); Flt Sgt C E Turner (Wireless Operator); Plt Off Jimmy Sukthanker (Navigator); Flt Sgt Jack Cooke (Navigator/Bomb Aimer); Plt Off Hugh Ashton (Rear air gunner); and Flt Lt 'Rick' Garvey, DSO, DFC (Skipper) in cockpit. A photo taken at Wyton in May 1943, 83 Squadron. The insignia – a red devil thumbing its nose, above the motto 'Devils of the Air' – was the first of three separate insignia applied to Queenie throughout her long operational career. The bomb log here shows 58 operations completed to date./H A Ashton, DFC

Below right: Rick Garvey (far left), who flew a total of 20 operations as skipper of Queenie with 83 Squadron, with his air and ground crews, Wyton, May 1943. Of the air crew; Jack Cooke (5th from left) eventually retired as Sqn Ldr, DFM; 'Freddie' Sukthanker, from India (8th from left) was awarded a DFC; Hugh Ashton (2nd from right) also received a DFC; whilst Bill Webster was killed in a flying accident. Garvey was later killed on operations. Of the 21 skippers who flew Queenie with 83 Squadron; nine were killed later on operations, and one who failed to return has an unknown fate. Two others have died since the war. / H A Ashton, DFC

units of the newly-created Path Finder Force.

The target selected for the PFF's first sortie was Flensburg on the night of August 18/19th. Six Lancasters from 83 Squadron were despatched (four others failed to take-off), including Queenie, with Ray Hilton at her controls, and 14 four-inch flares in the bomb bay. The raid proved to be a near-fiasco, at least as far as PFF was concerned. Of the 83 Squadron aircraft only two reported reaching the target, whilst Queenie, despite Hilton's deep experience, failed to locate the target and brought her flares back to Wyton. Hilton next took Queenie to Frankfurt on August 24/25th and released 112 x 30lb 'J' incendiaries across the city; but on Queenie's next operation – again against Frankfurt, on September 8/9th – Flight Sergeant L T Jackson and his crew suffered the frustration of being unable to locate the target. With the additional hazard of a complete failure of the crew intercomm system, Jackson brought his bomb load home. On September 13/14th, with Hilton back at her controls, Queenie flew to Bremen, carrying her first 4,000lb High Capacity (HC) bomb ('Cookie'). The following night Hilton was one of six 83 Squadron skippers despatched to Wilhelmshaven with a mixed load of HE bombs and flares. During the return trip Queenie was fired on by a 'four-engined night fighter' – a sarcastic description of a 'friendly' Lancaster by one of Queenie's crew – and the wireless operator, Flt Sgt Kitto was slightly wounded; a case of 'save me from my friends' . . .

During October 1942, Queenie flew only four operational sorties; against Krefeld, Aachen (when due to shocking visibility no attack was completed, and Queenie suffered hang-ups in the bomb release gear resulting in having to return with a 4,000lb 'Cookie' in her belly), Osnabruck and Kiel. On each of the latter three sorties the bomb load comprised a 4,000lb HC plus an assortment of marking and illumination flares. Such a load was hoisted into Queenie in the afternoon of November 6th, and just before 9.30pm that evening Ray Hilton pulled Queenie off Wyton's runway, bound for the long haul to Genoa, Italy. The sortie proved tragic for 83 Squadron. Of the 15 crews briefed, two were lost over the target, one crashed and blew up on landing back at Waterbeach, while a fourth Lancaster crashed landing at Mildenhall. All returning aircraft had been ordered to divert from Wyton, due to weather conditions, and Queenie, after more than nine hours airborne, landed safely at Mildenhall. Twelve hours later R5868 was again airborne, returning to Genoa, with Sqn Ldr J K M Cooke, DFC as skipper. The sortie was completed successfully despite heavy icing and frost over the Alps – or as the captain summed up, 'a sticky trip'.

As the result of a poor Met forecast on the night of November 9th, a projected raid on Hamburg ran into 10/10ths cloud conditions with strong winds, resulting in Ray Hilton releasing his 4,000lb 'Cookie' on Ratziburg instead. This particular operation is of importance in that one 'store' aboard Queenie was a Green Target Indicator (TI); though official sources have to date stated that Bomber Command's *first* use of TI's operationally was against Berlin on January 16/17th, 1943.

Three more hauls to Italian targets during November were undertaken by Queenie, in each case with different crews. On November 13th Hilton took a light load of HE bombs and flares to Genoa; whilst 48 hours later Plt Off R N H Williams, DFM took another mixed load to the same city, returned safely to Wyton, only to find the main runway blocked due to another Lancaster having collided with an Avro Anson 'hack' during landing. The third Italian operation was to Turin on November 29/30th when Flt Sgt H A Partridge and crew had a late take-off due to another 83 Squadron Lancaster, 'N' crashing and blocking the runway. Only two operations were undertaken by Queenie in December 1942. On December 3rd, in the early hours of the morning, Plt Off J Marchant, DFC, an

Left: Another pilot who flew Queenie on operations with 83 Sqn is Flt Lt M R Chick, DFC, who skippered the veteran over Germany on four occasions. Seen here in front of another 83 Sqn Lancaster, JA967, 'The Saint', Chick (centre rear) is seen with Flt Lt Drew and Warrant Officer Jack Slaughter; plus the faithful ground crew for JA967, at Wyton, January, 1944. /*Captain M R Chick*, DFC

Below: Squadron Leader Jack Partridge, DSO, DFC, who skippered Queenie on four of her operations, and later served at PFF headquarters./*Sqn Ldr J E Partridge*, DSO, DFC

83 Squadron crews after briefing, waiting outside a hangar for their transport to the aircraft, 1942.

Australian, captained Queenie to Frankfurt, and dropped his load of a 'Cookie' and ten 250lb incendiaries in 'one long stick' across the burning city from 16,500 ft. And on the night of December 21st Flight Lieutenant J Hodgson, DFC lifted a 'Cookie' to Munich, returning to Wyton just after 1 am the following morning. This Munich trip marked Queenie's 30th operation – the end of her first 'tour' of ops – and the air and ground crews accordingly 'awarded' Queenie a Distinguished Flying Cross (DFC), the ribbon of which was duly painted on her fuselage, just below the bomb log.

Queenie's first sortie against the 'Big City' (Berlin) came on January 16/17th, 1943. Loaded entirely with flares and TI markers, Queenie took off at 1655 hours with Ray Hilton once more at the controls – one of 201 bombers despatched that night. Unexpected haze and cloud over the target produced an anti-climax, though Hilton flew around the target area for 25 minutes. Unable to identify his marking point, Hilton brought his bomb load back. The same experience happened to Flt Sgt H A Partridge when he skippered Queenie's next operation. Despatched to bomb Wilhelmshaven on February 11/12th, Partridge found the target completely covered

by a cloud layer at 10-12,000 feet. Determined not to waste his trip, Partridge proceeded to release his 'Cookie' and three 500lb HE bombs on a sky marker. Below the cloud an ammunition depot at Mariensel received a direct hit and erupted in a series of gigantic explosions – a tribute to both the accuracy of the sky marking and Partridge's bomb aimer. Two nights later Flt Sgt Partridge bombed Lorient without incident; and the following night Sqn Ldr J K M Cooke returned to Italy, bombing Milan with a mixed load of HE bombs and TI's. On February 16th Queenie returned to Lorient with Sqn Ldr S Robinson, DFM as her captain. In spite of an unserviceable bombsight, the target was marked with white flares and red TI's, then bombed with a 4,000lb 'Cookie'. (Tragically, Robinson and four members of this night's crew were lost only 10 nights later).

Yet another skipper took the helm of Queenie on her next operation, Fg Off F J 'Rick' Garvey, who eventually was to complete 20 sorties as captain of R5868; more than any other individual pilot. The target was again Wilhelmshaven; the date February 18/19th, and Queenie was one of 195 bombers initially despatched. The following night Ray Hilton, now a Wing Commander, flew his 18th

sortie in Queenie, thereby completing his 27th operation of his second tour of ops. The target was Wilhelmshaven, and Hilton unloaded six 500lb HE bombs after releasing his red TI's. Ray Hilton, DSO, DFC after a few months 'rest' from operations, returned and was lost over Berlin during the night of 23/24 November 1943 – one of the PFF's early pioneers and most experienced leaders. Rick Garvey's next operation in Queenie, to Nuremberg, passed off without incident, but on the following night, February 26/27th, he was detailed for a raid on Cologne. The load comprised a 4,000lb 'Cookie' plus a dozen SBC's (Small Bomb Containers) each holding eight 30lb 'J' incendiaries. Over the target his bomb aimer, Sgt Jack Cook, released the load only to realise that the bombing electrical circuit was not functioning properly. The result was that the whole load was released on closed bomb doors, its total weight battering the doors open sufficiently to allow the bombs to drop away, but leaving the bomb bay doors partially open for the whole return trip and landing. One more raid in February – to St Nazaire on the 28th – was skippered by Plt Off V S Moore, DFM; but on March 5th Bomber Command flew the opening raid of the 'Battle of the Ruhr' – against Essen – as

the first sortie in a concentrated attack on German industrial targets.

Queenie's first sortie in this battle was to Nuremberg on March 8/9th, with Rick Garvey at the controls, as a backers-up bomber. Three nights later the same crew (with two exceptions) raided Stuttgart with a mixed load of flares, green TI's, bundles of 4lb incendiaries, and the now usual 4,000lb 'Cookie' as the 'ace in the hole'. Queenie's GEE set was useless and the mid-upper turret refused to function, but the sortie was duly carried out. Twenty four hours later Garvey and his crew in Queenie were sent to destroy the Krupps works at Essen – one of 457 aircraft despatched, 23 of which failed to return. On March 27/28th and 29/30th, Berlin was the target, with Garvey flying Queenie as one of the backers-up. On the second sortie they ran into trouble, being coned by probing searchlights, holed by flak, and then for some 12 minutes being chased by a Focke Wulf 190 and a Messerschmitt 110. By skilful co-operation between the gunners, Hugh Ashton (rear) and Stg L L J Thomas (mid-upper), Garvey was able to avoid their attacks and finally outdistanced the night-fighters.

For the following seven weeks, Q-Queenie

SILVER SHROUDS – a camera's view of Essen on the night of 3rd/4th April, 1943, from Lancaster 'V', 83 Squadron, whose pilot, Flt Sgt G A MacNichol, was commissioned but lost in action just two weeks later.

spent most of her time in the hangar, undergoing extensive servicing and general refurbishing; though first Flt Sgt G A McNichol piloted her to St Nazaire on April 2nd; one of his last sorties, because McNichol was killed in action on April 17th. Re-entering 'the lists' on May 23/24, Queenie – with Garvey at the controls – flew to Dortmund as a backer-up in the massive 826-aircraft raid that night; and on May 26th visited Dusseldorf. Next night Flt Sgt R King took Queenie to Essen with a full HE load and successfully bombed; though of the 518 aircraft despatched, 22 failed to return, whilst 107 others were damaged in varying degrees by the intense flak defences. On May 29th Fg Off M R Chick joined the lengthening list of Queenie's skippers with a sortie to Barmen-Wuppertal. The concentration of accurately-placed markers was reported as 'the best ever achieved to date' and resulted in the 700-plus bomber formations destroying over 1,000 acres of the target area. Chick's – and Queenie's – next successful operation was to Munster on June 11/12th – an exclusive PFF sortie in which 72 PFF aircraft were sent and caused 'considerable damage', according to the official report afterwards. A further sortie by Chick in Queenie followed the next evening, against Bochum, when 6,000lb of HE and 12 bundles of 4lb incendiaries were released on target accurately.

LOAD. A 4,000lb 'Cookie' nestles amongst a dozen 500lb MC bombs in the belly of Lancaster R5868.

Another captain, Flt Sgt M K Cummings, was at Q's controls on June 16th – a straight run to Cologne and back without interference from enemy defences. Next day Cummings was commissioned as Pilot Officer, whilst his rear gunner, Sgt R A Taylor was promoted to Flight Sergeant. Tragically, Cummings and his complete crew were lost on June 18th. This unhappy circumstance was repeated with Plt Off H Mappin and his crew, who flew Queenie's next operation on June 19/20th, against Montchanin. Two nights later Mappin and his crew (with one exception) failed to return from an operation over Germany, against Krefeld. That same night Fg Off Chick was back in Queenie's pilot seat and completed the Krefeld sortie without incident. On June 22nd Rick Garvey once more skippered Queenie in a raid on Mulheim, and two nights later bombed Elberfeld; followed by the first of a trio of trips to Cologne on June 28/29th, July 3/4, and July 8/9th. The second trip was Queenie's 60th operational sortie; accordingly the ribbon of a Distinguished Service Order (DSO) was added to the DFC award beneath her bomb log insignia. The third trip, on July 8/9th was not successful. Running into 10/10ths cloud, Garvey released his HE load blind through cloud; then had his windscreen holed by flak, and eventually came home with four Green TI's still aboard. This sortie was the 30th 'op' for Queenie's rear gunner, Hugh Ashton, and he was awarded a DFC soon after.

Italy was the target again when, on July 12th Fg Off W R Thompson piloted Queenie to Turin with a mixed load of HE and incendiaries; but on July 24th Bomber Command flew the opening 'round' of the Battle of Hamburg; sending 791 bombers and, incidentally, using the anti-radar foil, code-named 'Window', for the first time. That night Queenie was captain by Sqn Ldr R J Manton, a pre-war regular RAF pilot – later lost over Leipzig on October 20th, 1943. The following night – an OBOE and H2S-guided assault on Essen, – saw Rick Garvey acting as host to Brigadier-General Anderson of the USAAF, who went on the sortie ostensibly as second pilot; and the Group navigation officer, Sqn Ldr Price. The night of July 27th brought Garvey and Queenie, with Brig-General Anderson again, over Hamburg where the stricken city was bombed 'blind' on H2S-placed yellow TI's. Of the 787 bombers despatched that night, 17 failed to return. Two nights later Sqn Ldr Manton again captained Queenie to Hamburg, dropping a total of 9,000lb of HE into the holocaust below.

Queenie flew just two more operations with 83 Squadron PFF – both to Milan, and both in the capable hands of Rick Garvey. The first of these was on August 12/13th when Garvey was one of the backers-up aircraft; the second and ultimate sortie with the Pathfinders was flown on the night of August 14/15th, 1943, carrying four yellow TI's and 5,500lb of HE, and acting as visual marker over the aiming point. This sortie was the bomb aimer's (Flt Sgt Jack Cook) 35th operational sortie, and Rick Garvey's 20th at the helm of R5868. On August 16th, 1943, R5868, Q-Queenie left 83 Squadron for a complete overhaul at the maker's maintenance base. In all, Queenie had flown 67 operational sorties with 83 Squadron – an achievement proudly recorded on her fuselage bomb log, along with her DSO and DFC awards.

The subsequent history of R5868, though not within the context of this volume, is of particular interest from an historical viewpoint. In September 1943, R5868 was reallotted to 467 Squadron RAAF, stationed then at Bottesford, and commenced operations in her new guise as PO-S – 'Sugar' on the night of September 27/28th, 1943 with an attack on Hanover. Remaining with 467 until the cessation of hostilities in Europe, R5868 was finally flown to No. 15 Maintenance Unit, near Manchester, on August 23rd, 1945 and officially handed over to the 'civic authorities' (sic). During the period September 1943 to May 1945, R5868 flew a total of 68 sorties; thereby bringing her true war total to 135

operational trips. The credited total of 137 ops – still officially quoted – was the result of a simple clerical error during the first few weeks of her service with 467 Squadron; whilst other minor errors in later official records have tended to confuse the accurate history of this veteran Lancaster. Since the war, R5868 has had a chequered career; languishing in various Air Ministry maintenance units until 1959 when the aircraft was transferred to RAF Scampton, there to be erected, painted in her original markings as OL-Q of 83 Squadron, and being displayed in the open flanking the main entrance to the station. For the following 11 years Queenie bore the brunt of all weathers until November 24th, 1970 on which date she was dismantled and transferred to RAF Bicester for a complete refurbishment. Finally, R5868 was moved to her present home, the RAF Museum at Hendon, on March 12th, 1972. The only remaining puzzle is the official decision to have her restored in the markings of PO-S of 467 Squadron RAAF. With the fact that a genuine ex-operational Lancaster, W4783, ex-AR-G-George of 460 Squadron RAAF, is now in the Australian War Museum; it seems illogical that the Royal Air Force Museum should not mark the only genuine ex-operational Lancaster in the United Kingdom – and indeed, the sole surviving PFF aircraft – in its original RAF codings and insignia.

Queenie – a view taken just before completing its service with 83 Squadron.
/ H A Ashton, DFC

Left: On August 16th, 1943, Queenie was struck off the strength of 83 Squadron; was given a major inspection; then transferred to 467 Squadron RAAF at Bottesford, where she became coded PO-S. As 'Sugar', R5868 is seen here taking off from Waddington on night of May 11/12th, 1944 – reputedly (but incorrectly) attributed as the aircraft's 100th operational sortie.

Below left: R5868, PO-S, 467 Squadron RAAF, showing a bomb log of 137 operations. Crew here are, L-R: Flt Sgts Terry King; Harry Stubbs; George Wrightson; Fg Off Bob Swift (Skipper); Plt Offs John Lewis and Colin Wasson. The other figure is an unidentified administration officer, 'standing in' for the absent rear air gunner, Ken Symonds. This photo was taken in late April/early May 1945./R A Swift

Below: In contrast to the preceding photo is this view of R5868, PO-S, taken on May 7th, 1945, at the USAF fighter base at Kitzingen, north of Nuremburg; with its bomb log 'revised' to show only 125 operations. On this date S-Sugar was skippered by Wg Cdr I H A Hay on a recce for the 'Exodus' operation – the retrieval of Allied prisoners of war by air./A R T Boys, DFC

Bottom: MEMORIAL. R5868 as she is today, marked as PO-S, 467 Sqn RAAF, on permanent display in the RAF Museum, Hendon, near London, The 12,000lb HC bomb seen here under her belly was a store never lifted by R5868 throughout her long career./Ministry of Defence (Air)

Tales of the Crews

AIRBORNE – a Lancaster
leaves Mother Earth, bound
for a German target.

Virtually every man who flew operationally with the PFF could provide a lengthy story of his experiences. To tell every story is clearly impossible. And many stories of selfless sacrifice and superb courage can never be told; the men concerned did not survive to record their experiences. Nevertheless it is possible to illustrate something of the type of men these were; men who fought on to the very end, refusing to give up whilst there was even the slimmest chance of completing their given task. In RAF parlance such men were known as the 'Press-on' types. They were men not very different from their fellow crews; each was a human being unendowed with superhuman qualities, yet able to call on some unplumbed depths of determination and sheer courage when faced with seemingly impossible odds. Other men, not normally regarded as particularly aggressive, or of a 'press-on' nature, provided astonishing examples of raw bravery in the face of almost inevitable disaster. And through all such tales runs a common 'thread' – the priority concern of each man for the rest of his particular crew. The intimate 'togetherness' of each bomber crew was not simply a necessity of efficiency, though this was a prime consideration. It was equally a genuine feeling of brotherhood, created by the constant sharing of experience in facing possible death night after night. Seven or eight men, often with little else in common, were brought together –

often by sheer chance or circumstance – and quickly welded together into a team; efficient, self-reliant, interdependent, and led by a 'skipper' whose word was law in nearly all things. However well briefed and prepared prior to a sortie, once in the air it all depended on the individual crews whether the sortie was successful or not. Once airborne each crew was, in a sense, on its own. Decisions, adjustments, alterations to the planned operation were solely in the hands of each skipper.

The introduction, after August 1943, of a Master of Ceremonies – or Master Bomber, as he became titled – for specific heavy raids, bred a select type of skipper; very experienced, highly skilled, and cool under stress, and capable of directing the course of a raid involving many hundreds of aircraft over a single target. Amongst other facets, such a responsibility entailed lingering in the target area for longer periods than any other participating aircraft, with the consequent increased dangers from enemy defences. Three such Master Bombers were awarded posthumous Victoria Crosses. Others were men who had already completed two full tours of operations, yet had volunteered to continue flying operationally; in many cases completing over 100 sorties before being finally taken off 'ops'.

The following tales were selected to act as examples of the many other such stories that might be told of the PFF crews. Each exemp-

ARSE-END CHARLIE – the rear gunner of a Lancaster seated in his 'mighty Wurlitzer'. As here, many rear air gunners preferred to remove the centre perspex panel for clearer vision, and risk frostbite from the sub-zero temperatures of the upper night air.

lifies the spirit of the air crews, and each represents perhaps a hundred other similar stories that have never been told.

Hamburg was the target on the night of July 28/29th, 1944, and for Squadron Leader H F Slade, DFC of 156 Squadron this was to be the last op of his third tour. An Australian, and at 31 years, regarded by his crew as an 'old man', Slade reached the target approach, opened the bomb doors of his Lancaster, and commenced his bombing run-in to the target. Hit almost immediately by flak, his aircraft lost most of its port aileron, and a large chunk of the wing surface was bent upwards almost vertically, thereby acting as an air brake and making control difficult. Slade completed his bombing run, released the bombs, and turned for home. The Lancaster started a slow, spiral dive and, fighting to maintain control, Slade ordered his crew to stand by to bale out. Finally managing to get the bomber on an even keel, Slade set course for England with only 10 per cent aileron control. Crossing the enemy coast the Lancaster again came under fire from flak but Slade had little option but to fly straight through it. He was already losing height steadily and daren't put further stress on the crippled aircraft. Droning across the North Sea, Slade's flight engineer juggled with the remaining petrol to extract the last drop of endurance. The bomber continued to lose height and as it approached England, Slade requested an emergency clearance for a landing at Woodbridge, Suffolk. By the time he reached the airfield he was down to 1500 feet and therefore made a direct approach to land. Touching down at 140 knots, both wheels of the undercarriage burst and collapsed, partly due to flak damage, and the Lancaster skidded the length of the runway, shedding pieces along the way, but finally coming to a halt with its crew virtually unhurt. Slade was awarded an immediate DSO.

Flight Sergeant (later, Squadron Leader) Norman Francis Williams was also an Australian, from Leeton, New South Wales. An air gunner, he was serving on 35 Squadron, PFF in June 1943, and occupied his Halifax's rear turret for a raid on Dusseldorf. Despite a bright moonlit night, haze made general visibility difficult, but the Halifax reached its target and settled onto its bombing run-in. Williams immediately saw a German night fighter coming in from slightly above and on the port quarter. Swinging his turret, he opened fire at his attacker – and then '. . . the world fell on top of me'. A second fighter had come from under the bomber and raked the Halifax's fuselage with cannon fire. Williams was hit in the stomach by one shell; had his legs and thighs hit by either machine gun bullets or shrapnel; whilst one gun and the

turret mechanism was put out of action. Other damage caused included the mid upper gunner being hit in the head and temporarily blinded, and a cannon shell through the aircraft's starboard wing fuel tanks. The escaping petrol erupted in flames, leaving the Halifax as an illuminated target for further fighter and flak attacks. Paralysed below the waist, Williams, despite his pain, continued to give instructions to his skipper as both night fighters resumed their onslaught. Repulsing attack after attack, Williams found time to ask the bomb aimer to take the place of the wounded mid-upper gunner. No sooner was the latter in position than both German fighters bore in together from the port side. The Halifax banked away, and Williams' fire exploded one of the Germans. For the next few minutes nothing was seen of the second German. The bomb aimer resumed his normal duties and was replaced in the dorsal turret by the wireless operator. No sooner had he done so than the second German fighter appeared and attacked again. Finally, the fighter came in from dead astern. Williams, still partially paralysed and in great pain, waited until the German was at point-blank range, then fired. The fighter shed pieces of its fuselage and wings and disappeared under the Halifax. Other crew members reported it breaking up as it fell to earth. In all Williams and his fellow 'gunners' had fought off about 40 separate fighter attacks. Heading home, the

Inside view of the Frazer Nash FN20 rear turret. The twin depress-controls are seen at top of the control column; with firing thumb-buttons at centre-top. Below, left and right, are ammuniton boxes. At eye level, top, is the reflector gun sight, labelled 'Hands off'. The straps hanging from the doors were for flipping these closed – once in his seat, an air gunner had little room to move around.

skipper dived to extinguish the wing fire, and succeeded in doing this. Williams refused to leave his turret until the aircraft was clear of enemy territory, continuing to remain on the alert as the aircraft flew through coastal flak defences. Once over the North Sea, and comparatively 'safe', the other crew members tried to extricate the seriously wounded Williams from his turret, but its inner doors were jammed. Back at base the Halifax made a successful crash-landing, and Williams was chopped from his turret and taken to hospital. His courage earned him a Conspicuous Gallantry Medal. He later returned to operational flying, and was awarded a DFM in November 1943, followed by a Bar to his DFM in May 1944; thereby making him the most-decorated NCO of the RAAF in World War Two.

Wing Commander Basil Vernon Robinson was first commissioned in the RAF in 1933, and by September 1942 was commanding 35 Squadron, PFF. An experienced bomber captain, he had won a DFC with 78 Squadron prior to his appointment on 35 Squadron, and on the night of November 18/19th, 1942, was skipper of a Halifax acting as a marker for a main force raid against Turin in Northern Italy. One flare failed to release over the target and started burning in the aircraft bomb bay. Opening the bomb doors failed to disgorge the blazing pyrotechnic, and fire began to spread to the port wing. Robinson resigned himself to the inevitable and ordered his crew to bale out. As the last crew member obeyed his order, Robinson began to disentangle himself from the blazing bomber to take to his parachute – and, suddenly, the fire went out. A quick check confirmed that the flames were indeed extinguished. He was alone, in a partially crippled aircraft, some 700 miles from base, most of that distance being over hostile territory. It meant about four hours of flying the huge Halifax, without benefit of crew help in navigation, and protection from roving night fighters, but Robinson accepted the challenge. Crossing the Alps, he flew a direct route across occupied France to southern England, and eventually set the Halifax down on a fighter airfield – the first haven he could find. 'The look on the faces of the welcoming party (of ground crew) when just one man climbed out of the kite almost made the trip a pleasure', he is reported to have remarked later. Robinson was awarded a DSO for this singular feat of flying, and soon after was promoted to Group Captain and given command of RAF Graveley. Despite his new appointment, he insisted on flying further operations, and on the night of August 23rd, 1943, failed to return from a raid on Berlin.

John Fraser Barron, a New Zealander from Dunedin, was just 19 when he joined the

RNZAF in July 1940; a slight, modest boy, only five feet six inches in height. He arrived in England as a sergeant pilot in March 1941 – and within three years had become one of the PFF's veteran leaders, rising to Wing Commander and being awarded two DSO's, a DFC and a DFM. His first operations were with 15 Squadron, flying Short Stirlings by day and night against German and Italian targets. His early experiences included bombing the 'Happy Valley' (Ruhr) from 800 feet, and a particularly nerve-wracking trip to Genoa. Whilst crossing over Dunkirk on the outward trip of the latter sortie, his Stirling was hit by flak, which damaged the main bomb circuit electrics. Undeterred, Barron reached the target and attempted to bomb, only to realise that the 5,000 pounds weight of HE bombs in the fuselage refused to release. With this extra burden of weight, and in rapidly deteriorating weather, Barron started over the Alps for the return trip. Forced to detour from their original route because of the grim weather conditions, the crew soon realised that the remaining fuel was critical, and by the time the Stirling reached the Channel Islands the engineer reported to Barron that they had only 10 minutes flying time left. Without circuiting, Barron set the bomber down on the first airfield available, and as the Stirling settled on the runway, three engines spluttered and cut out – starved of fuel.

By March 1942 the young 'Kiwi' had completed 29 operations, but his 30th, a mine-laying sortie – was nearly his last. As the Stirling settled on its run-in to release its mine, light flak splashed along the fuselage, and one shell exploded inside, slashing the trimming wires and almost tearing the controls from Barron's grasp. With the help of a crew member, Barron got the aircraft home again, where a total of 97 shell-holes were counted in the bomber's fuselage. Completing 42 operations for his first tour, and having been awarded a DFM, Barron was commissioned and sent as an instructor for a 'rest'. Just four months later he came back to operations, again flying Stirlings to Italy. After a series of raids on Milan, Genoa and Turin, he was awarded a DFC. A trip to Munich on December 21st, 1942, proved to be decidedly 'dicey'. Barron was the first of the stream to bomb, and turned for home, only to be raked from end to end of the fuselage by a German night fighter. With his intercomm shot out, both gun turrets damaged, a fire in the rear fuselage, and the petrol cocks shattered, Barron finally evaded the fighter's onslaught and set a rough course for home. Reaching base, he then found that one of the Stirling's massive wheels would not come down. The engineer, Flight Lieutenant Robinson, managed to get the wheel down, and luckily, it held as the bomber touched down.

His 57th sortie was to Cologne, and during the run up to target, at 18,000 feet, his Stirling was coned by 'about 50 searchlights' – a perfect target for the flak guns, which quickly shattered the rear turret and damaged one propeller. Still coned – 'they lit us up for 16 minutes' – Barron completed his bombing and only then managed to get 'out of the limelight' by diving and turning away from the target. With compasses unserviceable, the Stirling was again fired on by flak over Ostend, but reached base eventually without further trouble. Shortly after, Barron received his third decoration, a DSO. The last sortie of Barron's second operational tour came on February 14th, 1943; a reasonably uneventful trip to Cologne; after which the young New Zealander returned to instructing. He remained on training duties until April 28th, 1944, on which date he was appointed as commanding officer of 7 Squadron at Oakington, flying Lancasters. On the night of May 19th, 1944, Barron was skipper of a Lancaster attacking marshalling yards at Le Mans – his 79th operational trip. Over the radio his voice was heard talking to another Lancaster captain, when a blinding flash lit up the sky – an air collision. Just 23 years old, and veteran of three years of war, John Fraser Barron did not live to wear the award of a Bar to his DSO promulgated after his death.

Above: Wing Commander John Barron, DSO, DFC (2nd from right) with one of his Stirling crews of 7 Squadron, Oakington./*Gp Capt T G Mahaddie*

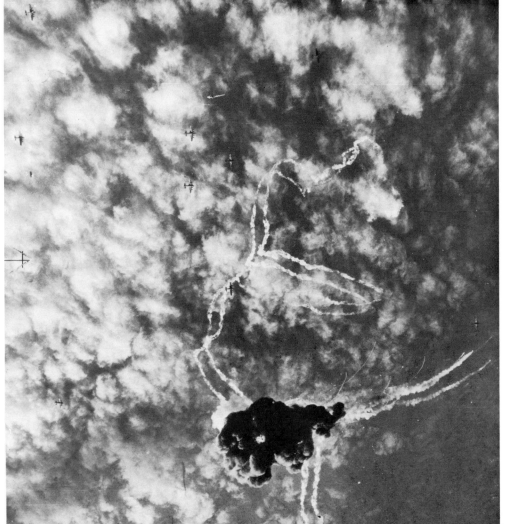

Left: THE MOMENT OF DEATH – a Lancaster explodes in the main stream, February 19th, 1945. Eight men have just died . . .

Left: A Halifax, its wing tanks ablaze, plunges onto the target, Gladbeck, on March 24th, 1945.

Top: ONE OF OUR AIRCRAFT IS MISSING . . . wreckage of a Short Stirling shot down by flak at Bremen on July 29th, 1942. / *Imperial War Museum*

Above: Tail section, minus gun turret, of a Lancaster which broke up over Berlin on August 31st, 1943./*Imperial War Museum*

147

Above: MASTER BOMBERS. Wing Commander Maurice Smith, DFC (far left); Flt Lt Page (Navigator); some ground crews, and (far right) Wing Commander John Woodroffe, DSO, DFC. Smith was selected as master bomber for the much-publicised raid on Dresden, on February 13th, 1945; the first of three raids within 14 hours that completely devastated the city and its inhabitants./*M A Smith*, DFC

Left: DRESDEN. A photo taken from a Lancaster of 156 Squadron, from 17,300 ft, at 0133 hrs on February 14th, 1945. The raid was only some three hours under way at this point, and fires were still mainly scattered.

Above right: DRESDEN – 2. The scene later – as the firestorm begins to reach its awful peak of intensity. One pilot reported, '. . . a sea of fire covering, in my estimation, some 40 square miles. The heat from the furnace below could be felt in my cockpit . . .'

Right: PATH FINDING FOR PEACE. Lancaster Z-Zebra of 635 Squadron, PFF, about to load British prisoners of war at Lubeck, on May 11th, 1945, bound for England. /*Imperial War Museum*

Gallery

A 635 Squadron Lancaster over the Normandy battle area on July 30th, 1944, viewed from 2,200 ft by Sqn Ldr Hugh Connolly, DFC, AFM, 635 Sqn.

Right: PFF LEADER – Don Bennett in a pensive moment.

Below: PFF PARTY. Wyton officers' Mess on a festive occasion.
Identifiable are: Wg Cdr John Northrop, DSO, DFC, AFC (left); Sqn Ldr N Bowman, DSO, DFC (2nd from left); Group Captain John Searby, DSO, DFC (3rd from left); Air Cdre C D C Boyce (4th from left); Grp Capt T G Mahaddie, DSO, DFC, AFC (seated front); Sqn Ldr 'Mickey' Finn, DFC (6th standing from left); Wing Commander George Grant, DSO, DFC (behind Finn).

Left: Wing Commander
Hugh Patrick Connolly, DFC,
AFM, who started his RAF
career as a Halton aircraft
apprentice; served at CFS;
saw operational service with
635 Squadron; and was Air
Commodore, Commandant
of Halton when he died in
1968./*Imperial War Museum*

Below left: Squadron Leader
C A J Smith, DFC of PFF
headquarters in late 1943.

Below: Group Captain S P
Coulson, DSO, DFC, who
commanded 582 Squadron
from December 1944./
Imperial War Museum

Far top left: Navigator – Flight Lieutenant Wilson, DSO, DFC.

Top left: Squadron Leader T ('Tommy') W Blair, DSO, DFC & Bar, who flew 100 operations. On at least 50 of these, he took with him his pet cocker spaniel dog, 'Sammy'./*Imperial War Museum*

Far left: Wing Commander G H Womersley, DSO, DFC, who commanded 139 (Mosquito) Squadron in 1944.

Left: Wing Commander T W Horton, DSO, DFC & Bar, who flew with 105 Squadron at one period. A New Zealander, born in Masterton, he was a law clerk before joining the RNZAF in October 1939.
/ *Imperial War Museum*

Above: 'DOC' – Wing Commander J C MacGown, MD, Ch B, the 8 Group senior medical officer. An ex-Royal Flying Corps fighter pilot of 1917-18, Mac flew a total of 52 PFF operations with various crews '. . . for usefulness of medical gen on the crews!' He was deservedly awarded a DFC for his operational career.

Right: Squadron Leader Howard Lees, 8 Group Photographic Officer. His many ideas and practical inventions included the 'master' and 'slave' cameras, which eliminated fire tracks caused by the open shutters of normal night cameras; thereby obtaining clear, undistorted target photos for analysis.

Above: Wing Commander (later, Air Commodore) J E Fauquier, DSO, DFC, who commanded 405 Squadron RCAF in its first nine months of operations.

Above right: Squadron Leader R A 'Wimpy' Wellington, DSO, DFC, who served with 83 Squadron, PFF.

Right: Flight Lieutenant J C Wernham of 405 Squadron, RCAF, who was shot down in Germany on March 30th, 1944. He was sent to the infamous Stammlager Luft 3, where he took part in the 'Great Escape'. Recaptured, he was one of 47 officers ruthlessly shot by the Germans shortly after.

Above: Squadron Leader A F Chisholm, DFC of PFF headquarters staff in 1943.

Above right: Wing Commander R P Elliott, DSO, DFC, who commanded 627 Squadron 1942-43; then became station commander at Upwood in 1943, and commanded the PFF Navigation Training Unit at one period.

Right: Squadron Leader A C Douglass, DFC of 105 Squadron.

Left: Wing Commander J R G 'Roy' Ralston, DSO, AFC, DFM, who was another ex-Halton aircraft apprentice. From sergeant pilot on Blenheims, he graduated' to Mosquitos with 105 Squadron; had a spell at PFF HQ; and finished the war as commander of 139 Squadron. /*Imperial War Museum*

Below left: Squadron Leader Ian Willoughby Bazalgette, VC, DFC. Born in Calgary, Alberta, Canada, he came to England as a boy, and in July 1939 joined the Royal Artillery, being commissioned the following year. Transferring to the RAF in September 1941, he subsequently saw operational service with 115 Squadron and was awarded a DFC. He joined 635 Squadron in April 1944. On August 4th, 1944, skippering Lancaster B.III, ND811, 'F2-T', Bazalgette was master bomber for a raid on Trossy St Maximin – a daylight sortie. Attacked by fighters which set his Lancaster on fire, and seeing his deputy master bomber shot down, Bazalgette continued his marking and bombing run. Then, with his bomb aimer critically wounded, and the burning bomber losing height, he ordered the crew to bale out. Bazalgette, however, attempted to land in order to save his wounded crew member. The Lancaster exploded and crashed near Senantes, France. A posthumous VC was gazetted on August 17th, 1945./*Imperial War Museum*

Below: Squadron Leader Robert Anthony Maurice Palmer, VC, DFC. Born in Gillingham, Kent, Robert Palmer joined the RAF Volunteer Reserve in late 1938, and in November 1940 joined 75 (NZ) Squadron, flying Wellingtons. After only three operations, he was posted to 149 Squadron, with which unit he finished his first tour of ops. After a long period of instructional duties (during which he managed to fly several operational sorties), he joined 109 Squadron in August 1943. During the following year he was awarded a DFC and Bar, and completed an overall total of 100 operations. On December 23rd, 1944, Palmer was selected as master bomber for a daylight raid on Cologne marshalling yards. Instead of his customary 109 Sqn Mosquito, he chose to fly a 582 Sqn Lancaster, PB371, '60-V', and took his navigator from 109 and 582 Sqn members for the rest of his crew. Hit by flak a few minutes before the target Palmer's Lancaster had two engines set on fire, but with smoke and flames filling the fuselage, he continued his bombing run. Attacked by Luftwaffe fighters as he neared the target, he completed his run and bombed. Almost immediately his Lancaster was seen to spiral in flames to the ground; only one crew member escaped from the doomed aircraft. His posthumous award of a VC was gazetted on March 23rd, 1945. His final sortie was his 110th operation.

Left: Captain Edwin 'Ted' Swales, VC, DFC, SAAF. Born in Inanda, Natal, South Africa, Swales enlisted in the South African Army in June 1935; and when war broke out in 1939, fought in Ethiopia, and later through the North African desert campaigns as a Warrant Officer. After Montgomery's Alamein offensive in 1942, Swales returned to his native land and transferred to the SAAF. In August 1943 he was seconded to the RAF, and eventually joined 582 Squadron at Little Staughton in mid-1944. His eighth operation was on the same raid in which Ian Bazalgette died. On December 23rd, 1944 – his 33rd sortie – he was in the bomber formation led by Sqn Ldr Robert Palmer raiding Cologne. Attacked five times by Luftwaffe fighters, Swales' coolness under fire permitted his gunners to destroy at least one German fighter; and he was awarded a DFC. On the night of February 23rd/24th, 1945 – his 43rd operational sortie – Swales was selected as master bomber for a concentrated attack on Pforzheim. Flying Lancaster PB538, '60-M', Swales was attacked over the target by a Messerschmitt Bf 110, whose fire shattered one engine and holed the fuel tanks. Continuing his bomb run, Swales was again hit by the night fighter, which knocked out a second engine. Completing his duties, Swales turned for home but his crippled Lancaster steadily lost height. Finally Swales ordered his crew to bale out, but remained at his controls in order to give them the best chance of escaping. The aircraft nosed into some high tension cables and exploded. For his selfless sacrifice, attempting to save his crew, Swales was awarded a posthumous VC on April 24th, 1945 – the only SAAF member ever to receive this supreme honour. /*Imperial War Museum*

Below: Flight Lieutenant Walter Reif (centre), with Flight Sergeant G Owen (left) of his crew, and Owen's brother, Sub-Lieutenant Les Owen. Reif, a pilot on 582 squadron, took off right behind Sqn Ldr Bob Palmer on the latter's final sortie of December 23rd, 1944. He, and his crew, failed to return./*L Owen*

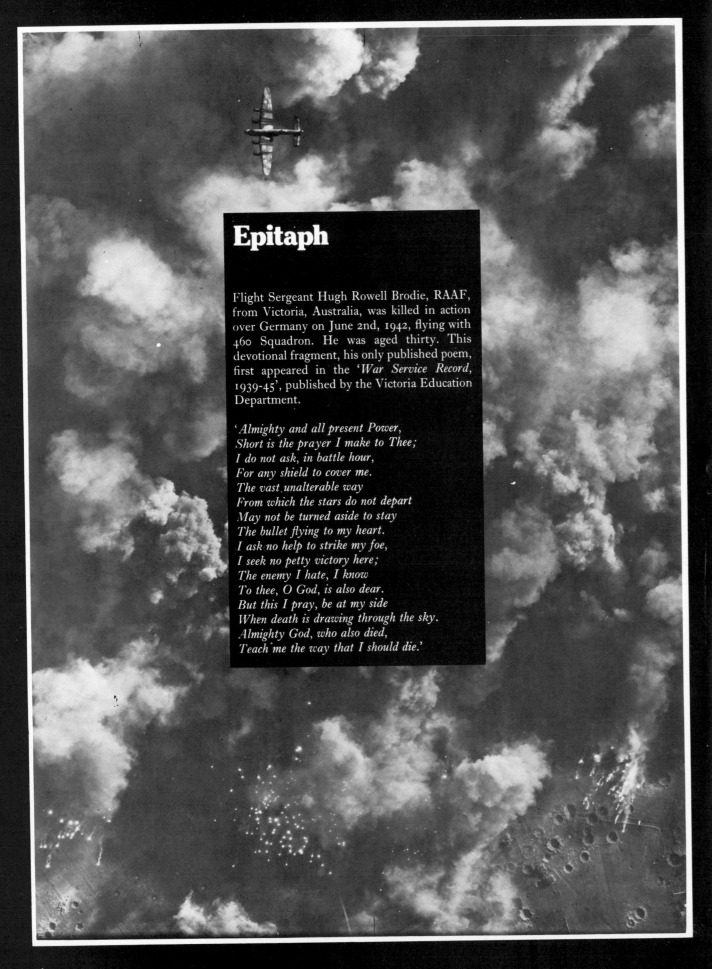

Epitaph

Flight Sergeant Hugh Rowell Brodie, RAAF,
from Victoria, Australia, was killed in action
over Germany on June 2nd, 1942, flying with
460 Squadron. He was aged thirty. This
devotional fragment, his only published poem,
first appeared in the 'War Service Record,
1939-45', published by the Victoria Education
Department.

'*Almighty and all present Power,*
Short is the prayer I make to Thee;
I do not ask, in battle hour,
For any shield to cover me.
The vast unalterable way
From which the stars do not depart
May not be turned aside to stay
The bullet flying to my heart.
I ask no help to strike my foe,
I seek no petty victory here;
The enemy I hate, I know
To thee, O God, is also dear.
But this I pray, be at my side
When death is drawing through the sky.
Almighty God, who also died,
Teach me the way that I should die.'